Saved for Success

A Guide For Living In The Grace Of God

Rev. LeRoy Thompson, Ph.D.

· Chicago ·

Saved for Success

A Guide For Living In The Grace Of God

Rev. LeRoy Thompson, Ph.D.

Published by
Joshua Tree Publishing
• Chicago •
JoshuaTreePublishing.com

All rights reserved. No part of this book may be reproduced or transmitted in any form or by any means, electronic or mechanical, including information storage and retrieval system without written permission from the publisher, except by a reviewer who may quote brief passages in a review.

13-Digit ISBN: 978-1-941049-97-6

Copyright © 2020. Rev. LeRoy Thompson, Ph.D. All Rights Reserved.
Cover Photo: Copyright © 2020. Rev. LeRoy Thompson, Ph.D.

All Bible verses are from the King James Version (KJV) Public Domain

Disclaimer:
This book is designed to provide information about the subject matter covered. The opinions and information expressed in this book are those of the author, not the publisher. Every effort has been made to make this book as complete and as accurate as possible. However, there may be mistakes both typographical and in content. Therefore, this text should be used only as a general guide and not as the ultimate source of information. The author and publisher of this book shall have neither liability nor responsibility to any person or entity with respect to any loss or damage caused or alleged to be caused directly or indirectly by the information contained in this book.

Printed in the United States of America

Dedication

This book is for my wife, Rita. She is the most wonderful wife, lover, companion, friend, sister in the Lord, and partner in crime. She also saved my life, twice—once by leading me by example into a personal relationship with the Lord, and the second time by shining her light so that I could find my way through my darkest days.

Table of Contents

Preface 7
Chapter one: Some Foundation Truths 11
Chapter Two: Developing Unconscious Competence 25
Chapter Three: Living by Revelation 43
Chapter Four: Practical Application 59
Epilogue 103
About the Author 104

Preface

When you have been so richly blessed in life, you feel compelled to help others. And in so doing, you add to your blessings. This is a faith-based book. The ideas and tools come directly from my experience as a Christian and are tested by the guidance that the Bible has provided. It's important to me, though, to avoid "church speak." Rather I will provide enough scriptural references and a few study challenges to encourage you to dig deeper. My hope, though, is that the notion of faith will be even more relevant to you as a practical matter of living successfully and not the obligatory duty to which I feel much of the church world has already devolved. And if my heart of love and compassion for you, your life, and the life of your family does not become obvious to you as you read, then I have failed well beyond neglecting to quote an abundance of scriptures. Although it was essential for me to process scriptural wisdom on my own terms and in my own language, it was also other people who sowed into me these seeds of wisdom. And I'm encouraging you to do the same. Take what is shared here to heart, not only because it works but also to develop your own template for how to apply it. And after you have seen the benefits of that wisdom, make an effort to pass it along to someone else. That is how the world becomes a better place—sharing our abundance with others. In 2 Timothy 2:2, Paul told Timothy to take the lessons that were passed on to him and share them with others who would, in turn, share them again, and so on.

Let me also say a quick word about the idea of success. I've had way too many people object to this book even before I wrote it just because of the title! Success to me is a compendium. Sure, it can include financial well-being, but that is near the bottom of the list. Being healthy, being loved, feeling as if you've made a difference—these and many other things end up way ahead of money. (In fact, money will be the last thing we talk about here.) It's up to each of us to define what the ingredients are that add up to success. What I will suggest to you is that, in addition to a list of good things, real success is when all those things are adding strength, energy, and joy to your life and working together to make your life whole.

There are two words used in the Bible that say this so very much better than I can. The Shema is a prayer that begins in Deuteronomy 6:4. It says that the Lord is "one." This is not the number one but the word *echad*. It is a very complex concept. Minimally, it expresses that the idea of the essence of God, who, being infinitely complex, unifies absolutely everything and brings it together in a simple oneness. The second is the word *shalom*. When Jesus greeted the disciples after his resurrection in John 20:21, he told them "Shalom aleichem," or "Peace be unto you." The best translation of the word *shalom* is actually "wholeness." The culturally common greeting "Shalom aleichem" can mean "Hello," "Goodbye," "How are you?" "Have a nice day," and more. Jesus, though, was literally blessing them by saying, "May wholeness [shalom] be like bread [aleichem] to you." What is actually being conveyed in the greeting is a wish that wholeness feeds you.

Success is when everything in your life is working together as *echad*, flowing in seamless unity, *shalom*. Success is wholeness. It is the contentment that feeds everything going on in you and around you. This book is designed to help you live out the unity and wholeness of your salvation. And if you happen to read this book and do not know the Lord, it would be an even greater outcome that you would be drawn to accept Jesus as your Lord and Savior.

The design of this book is straightforward, I hope. In the first three chapters, we'll begin by looking at some foundational truths, some fundamental mindsets, and then some deeper spiritual insights that underlie our ability to rejoice in our salvation. What I have seen, in over thirty-five years of ministry, is that too many people are not cognizant of their own underlying assumptions and the lens through which they filter all their experiences, including their relationship with the Lord. From that point forward, we'll address the application of those truths and insights to the activities of our daily lives, such as work, career, marriage, family, and even parenting. We'll look at several "case studies" throughout as well. These are drawn from people I have encountered and have asked if we can share the story of their journey with you.

Enjoy, and I hope the truth and wisdom you find here will feed you every day as if it were bread.

Chapter One

Some Foundation Truths

I want to share with you three foundational truths upon which the other ideas in this book will stand:

1. Understanding the purpose for which the Lord saved you
2. Recognizing that you were specifically chosen by God to fulfill that purpose
3. Living in the reality of unconditional love and acceptance

Purpose: My Story

The first truth is to appreciate the continuity of your existence. Your purpose and destiny have been unfolding at every turn along the way. Not much (if anything) has been random or coincidental. Even the worst things that have happened have had a productive influence on where you are headed. The best way I know to convey it is to tell you a little bit about my journey. Rather than bore you to tears with my entire life story, let me capture a few salient sound bites that will make the point. I have only been able to trace the seeds of my success as far back as the early 1800s in the areas of Pageton, West Virginia; Ajax, Virginia; and Tazewell County, Virginia.

I have particular knowledge of the Edwards side of the family and credit much of who I am to my grandfather Samuel Petress Edwards, who eventually settled in Bluefield, West Virginia, in the early 1920s. His grandparents Wesley and Patience Edwards were born in 1830 and 1829, respectively, and lived in the area of Ajax, Sandy Level, Virginia (about sixty miles south of Roanoke, Virginia). They were both free African Americans. Wesley was a farmer and tobacconist owning nearly five hundred acres of land. In addition to the farm, Wesley and Patience operated a retail store in Pittsylvania County, Virginia. Wesley and Patience gave birth to John Wesley Edwards, who married Emma. John and Emma gave birth to Bertie C., Walter, Luke, and Samuel Petress. John Wesley Edwards was also free, and he and Emma operated a brickkiln business. John Wesley passed away in 1900, the year Granddaddy was born.

Granddaddy was a great storyteller and loved to sit me on his lap and lull me with his mesmerizing recollections. But they weren't just stories. Each one seemed to have a point, and I always felt I had been taught a gentle lesson as his last words would always be "So now, Rockyman, do you understand what I'm telling you?" (He called me Rockyman. My nickname was Rocky. I was born a month and a half late and weighed eleven pounds, fourteen ounces when I came out. My Mom and I almost did not survive birth. She was in the hospital for six months, and I was there for three. When they allowed to me to go home, the story is my grandmother, Gammy, held me and said, "Boy, you sure had a rocky road to travel.")

He told me stories about how his Dad regularly bought food to give to his poorer neighbors. Each ended with "So now, Rockyman, do you understand what I'm telling you?" He told me about when he was a young man and left to see the world and set out for New

York City, of all places. When he had trouble finding work, he pretended to speak Spanish and got a job as a Pullman train porter. Every night he would hang out with the other Latino workers and learn enough of the language to keep the job. ("Rockyman, do you understand what I'm telling you?") By far, his favorite story was recounting the battle between David and Goliath. He shared it in great detail and with a lot of passion and enthusiasm. He would talk so much about how strong Goliath was that every time he told it, I felt like David was going to lose. But every time David won, and Granddaddy would ask me how he did it? "God picked him to win," I learned to repeat. ("So now, Rockyman, do you understand what I'm telling you?") Among the most precious things that my grandfather passed along to me was the idea that all of us have a special purpose in life.

"Everyone has a place," I remember him telling me, "and you've got to give yourself the chance to find yours." ("So now, Rockyman, do you understand what I'm telling you?")

Although it took me decades to really understand what he meant, it was his actions that made such an indelible imprint on my mind. You see, Granddaddy knew that his place was to make sure that his children found their place, and so he did whatever he had to do to propel my mom, Aunt Loretta, and Uncle Randy beyond the abject poverty that surrounded us in the Appalachian Mountains. When he moved to Bluefield, Granddaddy worked as a coal miner. Every day at 4:30 a.m., he and his fellow miners took turns being lowered down on a rope nearly a mile under the mountain. For ten hours, they would chop, scrape, and dig away at the walls, working in a space not much larger than the inside of your car. Every Christmas, when the mine gave its workers huge bushel baskets of fruits and nuts as their bonus, he and I would carry them around to share with needy neighbors.

My mom and dad grew up together in Bluefield and were childhood sweethearts. When she was just thirteen years old at Genoa Junior High School, Mom began telling her girlfriends that when she grew up, she would have a son, and he would go to Harvard. (Not many of her friends had much expectation of escaping Bluefield, and even fewer knew what Harvard was!) Both of my parents managed to "escape" in the 1950s after becoming college graduates. They moved to Baltimore to find work and left me with my grandparents until I was five. Although my parents were both public school teachers, they determined to put me in private school. I started first grade surrounded by mostly Jewish kids from some of the wealthiest families in Baltimore. As a "cultural amphibian," I divided my time between them, my lower-middle-class neighborhood in Baltimore, and summers in the mountains of Bluefield. I was never confused about my identity, but it was necessary to learn how to navigate these incredibly diverse social environments. As an accomplished athlete, I became part of an elite boys' club that toured each summer, playing sports and living with families in South America, Europe, Asia, and Australia. And yes, I did end up at Harvard.

After I graduated, I, too, was off to see the world and landed in Chicago. (Boy, do I still love Chicago!) My first job was a commercial banker, and one morning, I was sitting at my desk and saw this young woman walking down the hallway. After I picked my jaw off the ground, I called my best friend and told him I had met "her" (guy code for the woman of your dreams). He asked me who she was, and I told him I didn't have the faintest idea! When I finally met her, we became great friends (not what I was looking for, by the way). But she was just such a wonderful person, so I was good with that. Once, while talking about our anticipated futures, she confided in me that she knew that she was destined to run for political office and marry a pastor. That clearly took me out of the running, but our friendship continued to grow. Amazingly, the friendship turned to love, and she and I were soon married! Honestly, I am still blown away that someone as kind, beautiful, and powerful as she would want me.

Soon after, we gave birth to a son and a daughter, and I started my own consulting business. Then we started going to this church. I had one major epiphany after another and became deeply involved in the congregation, eventually becoming a part of the leadership as an elder. Unfortunately, the pastor became seriously ill and, even after recovering, was not able to continue in his role.

Can you see what's about to happen next? Exactly. I was asked, along with Rita, to take over the congregation and be the pastor!

I could keep going on like this for another five pages, but I hope you get the message. The footprint for my success was established in the generations that came before me, and the plan for my destiny has been woven from every life experience that has come my way. This is the first and most important lesson that successful people learn. Stop for a bit and look back to see how you got where you are now. You will begin to see a clear path back and, most likely, a collection of precious people who have contributed to you being there. And if by chance, you don't feel you are in the right place, look closer to see where you diverged, and realign yourself.

Chosen-ness

I have encountered at least two categories of people—those who strive for success from the point of view of convincing themselves that they deserve it, and those who are just simply convinced of their success. I'm not going to say that there aren't some successful people in the first category. I will say that (1) there are far fewer than in the second, (2) they struggled significantly more to obtain that success, and (3) they are more likely to see their success as a fleeting accomplishment rather than a state of being.

One of the great blessings of going to school with the Jewish kids was learning some of the depth of their culture. I will *never* forget a conversation I had with a group of classmates sometime around fifth or sixth grade. On the playground one day, we were all talking about what we were going to do when we grew up. One of the other non-Jewish kids made a comment about hoping one day to be fortunate enough to be successful, not necessarily rich or famous like a movie star but just successful. You should have seen the looks on the faces of our eleven- and twelve-year-old Jewish colleagues. Every one of them had this weird expression of utter confusion and bewilderment. As they momentarily revealed to us, they had all been raised with the clear understanding that they had already been predestined to be successful people! They were shocked that one would actually wonder about something like that. They were not conceited or arrogant about this. They did not consider themselves better than the rest of us. They just had been raised to see success as a natural consequence of being who they were. They were chosen.

Here is the second foundational truth. You may not be Jewish either, but I'm hoping something just began to stir in your heart. I'm hoping you began to realize that what had been passed on to them is common to all of us regardless of your ethnocultural heritage. I can tell you that it hit me hard enough to have left a permanent imprint on my psyche. There is something deep within me that knows (not just believes but knows) that I have been *chosen* to fulfill my particular destiny. I can certainly anchor this to my own faith, but my faith also confirms that this is a foundational truth for all of us. "Chosen-ness" affects your life in at least five profound ways:

The Five Gifts of Chosen-ness

It boosts your resilience in the face of life's difficulties. When you understand the concept of intrinsic purpose, anything and everything can ultimately be seen as contributing toward that purpose. This will be true whether or not it seems so at the time you are encountering it.

It creates a "wealth mentality" whereby there is always enough. You will always have enough—enough time, enough money, enough love, enough patience, and enough courage. Most people have a "poverty mentality." There is *never enough* no matter how much they have. This breeds an inherent discontent that is not easily erased no matter how many good things may be happening.

It takes care of the self-esteem problem that so many people suffer from. Your source of esteem becomes internal rather than external. I don't need a reason to feel good about myself. Being me is a good thing in and of itself. I'm not better than anyone and don't need to be to feel good about who I am. If you don't esteem *yourself,* why would anyone else be inclined to either?

It teaches you to give and to serve others, which in turn enriches your own life. There are irrefutable properties of the universe whereby the act of giving (or taking) returns to the sender. The more you give, the more is given to you. Fascinatingly enough, what comes back to me is often not the same thing that I gave, but it's generally something I needed.

It allows you to live in peace. Stay with me here for a second. Anger is obviously one of the most potentially destructive human emotions, right? Anger, most often, is born from fear. We become angry when what we expect, want, or need is threatened. We direct anger at other people as a way of keeping them from becoming (or continuing) to be a threat to us. When you have received the first four gifts of chosen-ness you live with a lot less fear. In fact, not only is there less need for anger; but resentment, frustration, jealousy, and envy also don't have a foothold on you. In other words, the likelihood of me not having what I expect, want, or need is far less likely because I am carrying around most of it inside me. And if I'm not walking around all the time protecting myself, anger is less of a necessary emotion to maintain my sense of equilibrium as a person.

My grandfather never felt that his lot in life was an accident. Granddaddy intrinsically knew that he was chosen and never once resented occupying the space he was given. It was acceptable to him to be lowered into a dark, choking, methane-infused pit ten hours a day so that his kids could rise to the heights of their potential for the rest of their lives. In my opinion, your life is not an accident either, and you are not powerlessly ping-ponged by some random state of events *unless* you merely want to live that way. The truth is that you, too, are chosen, and if you haven't been acting that way, now is the time to begin.

Unconditional Acceptance

There is no other way to say this, so here goes: Much of what people have been taught about God, Jesus, the Holy Spirit, salvation, etc. is VASTLY different from what the Bible actually says. This is true both in the meaning of individual passages of scripture and in the warp and woof of the major themes that run throughout both the

Old and the New Testaments (covenants, more precisely). I'll treat these theological subjects lightly so as not to stray too far from the main point here, but it is essential to understand a little of this to grasp the basics. In all honesty, what I really want to do is to make sure that those of you reading this who have been on the fence about Jesus will get a better slant on things than what you might have been told or read. I don't want to offend anyone, but what the institutional church has done to pervert the truth of the gospel is criminal. We simply must let people know the truth.

God Is Not Mad at You

For one, God is not mad at you. I know that's a shocker because the foundation of much religious practice is for you to find ways to atone for your wretchedness in hopes of not spending an eternity burning in hell. The notion of your despicableness in the sight of God has been nearly indelibly etched into the minds of the vast majority of people, whether they have accepted Jesus as their Savior or not. The problem is that it is not true to the extent that you may have been taught. The most profound concept in the New Covenant is that God made the decision to love and accept you even before you knew about him. At this moment, you're likely expecting me to give you a boatload of scriptures and biblical examples to prove my point. But I'm not going to do that. I'm simply going to plead with you to begin reading the Bible with that possibility in mind and see for yourself how much overwhelming confirmation you will find for the presupposition. You see, whenever we consider an idea, we always have a basic supposition that our brain uses the frame and classify the new information. If your supposition is that God is mad at you, you will synthesize that fact from whatever you read. When you encounter contradictions to your supposition, you will be forced to overlook or rationalize them because your supposition is your guiding principle. Are there apparent contradictions to the idea that God is not mad at you? Of course, the scriptures are deep and often murky. The point is that there are so few contradictions for that position compared with the ridiculously long list of contradictions, logical fallacies, and cognitive dissonance that you will need to construct to justify the idea that God hates you. Try John 3:16–17 right now and see what I mean. (Yes, read it *right now*.) If you want to maintain the prevailing religious supposition, then you're suggesting that this passage says "God so loved the world that he sent his beloved son Jesus to redeem those who he created but hated them so much, he wants to destroy them." If that's the case, then either you or God is confused. (Sorry, gonna have to go with God on this one!)

What Is Salvation and Why Do I Need a Savior?

Because of this misguided indoctrination, it's hard to see the need for a Savior. This is why I believe that record numbers of people who confess to believe are staying away from churches in droves. How long can you listen to someone tell you how rotten you are, especially when you are already painfully aware of your shortcomings? Going to church and knowing that "Captain Obvious" will be preaching just gets old (and is debilitating to your heart). We know we have problems, and what we're most in need of is answers. We know we're lost, but what would be nice would be some easy directions. The gospel keeps getting labeled as the "good news," but in so many of our churches, radio programs, and TV shows, where, oh where is the good news? Simply put, the gospel says that Jesus's mission was to restore your true identity in God and bring you back to the state of innocence in which you were originally conceived. In other words, religious people have been telling us that humanity was a *problem* that God had to solve by sending a savior. What the Bible really says is that you and I are the *solutions* to a preexisting problem. It took God coming in the form of humanity to enable us to understand how we were created to be. The life of a believer is never about worrying if God will wipe you out. He had the chance if that's what he wanted to do. No, a believer's life is about understanding the purpose for which we were saved.

> **Study Challenge:**
>
> If you want to grasp this, then read the first three chapters of the Book of Genesis in a translation that uses the original meaning. It'll blow you away.

Blame It All on Constantine (and Maybe Dante Too)

For many of you, what I have just been saying seems like pure fantasy. I get it. The church and everyone else has been un-biblically-indoctrinated for over 1,700 years! Pick up any credible book on church history, and you can verify all this for yourself. Believers from the time of Jesus until the mid-300s met in houses, fellowshipped daily, paid no attention to titles, and were in a constant learning mode, discovering what it meant to be chosen by God. When Constantine defeated Maxentius and then Licinius, he became the sole leader of the Roman Empire. He issued the Edict of Milan in 313 AD, making "Christianity" the official religion of what would be called the Holy Roman Empire. The good news was that three hundred years of gruesome persecution against believers came to an end. The consequence was the formalization of the faith. This quickly resulted in separating those in ministry from the people they served and elevating ministers to a religious and political status that virtually sucked the spirituality out of what it had meant to follow Jesus. Reading and interpreting the scriptures becomes the sole province of a now-professional clergy. Elaborate robes and garments, looking down at the congregation from pulpits built high above them, paying for salvation and forgiveness, and so many other aberrations found their way into the life of believers. Eventually, church became somewhere you *go* rather than *the people* themselves. So you can blame Constantine for the chaos of what we have come to call Christianity.

Another huge contribution to the chaos came from Dante Alighieri, a thirteenth-century Italian Renaissance poet. He penned the famous work traditionally entitled *Inferno*. Technically the work was called *Divine Comedy*, a series of journeys he takes with his spiritual guides, the Roman poet Virgil and his love interest, Beatrice. He visits hell, purgatory, and paradise. He depicts hell as having nine different layers based on the type of sin that has been committed. At each level, the sin and the fiery punishment gets worse and worse. Ultimately one can climb out of hell into purgatory by climbing down the body of Lucifer. It is said that the power of Dante's sacred poem in popularizing this theology and philosophy, still at the present day, is almost "incalculable." In other words, the institutional church promoted Dante's view of hell so widely and deeply that it became "what the Bible said" rather than a creative work of literature. It was even penned in common Italian rather than in traditional Latin so that it could be even more widely accepted. Here again, what the Bible says about hell is far different. If your theology was rocked by what we've already been talking about, you don't want to hear about hell!

Religion Versus Relationship

I really am going somewhere practical and valuable with all this historical stuff. At the end of the day, being "saved for success" is all about the practical value of faith. I just need to make sure you understand these in order for you to derive that value in your daily life. You see, faith is not at all about going to church, reading the Bible, saying your prayers, or any of the long list of actions in which you will see believers engaged. We go to church, read the Bible, say our prayers, and all those other things *because* we have a vibrant relationship with God. We go to church, read the Bible, say our prayers, and all those other things through a vibrant relationship based on the identity and innocence that faith in what Jesus has done provides. A *vibrant* relationship. A 365-24-7 open line of contact, communication, and communion with the deep spiritual dimension that exists within us. There is a *huge* difference between doing all these things because you believe God requires them as a condition of salvation, love, and acceptance versus doing them joyfully and purposefully because you are already saved, loved, and accepted. A *huge* difference. Once again, start with that supposition, and read books like 1 and 2 Corinthians, Ephesians, Romans, or Hebrews. Everything is in the past tense, already done, finished. The task is to live in the reality of that finished work. If not, much of what we'll get into in the remainder of this book will be twice as hard to understand and half as useful. There's a power to this idea of grace that will enable you to live a richer, more complete, more rewarding, and purposeful life. If you find yourself loving and accepting yourself, it will be a lot easier loving and accepting others. If you have trouble loving and accepting yourself, then you are a target for guilt and then a sitting duck for shame. Guilt and shame are the two worst things that can happen to a person and the two most important things that grace triumphs over.

Case Study: A Tale of Two People

Rita and I have known Lynette, her husband, Richie, and their four kids for almost thirty years. She, in particular, is just a nice person. She's attractive, kind, warm, and welcoming to anyone she meets. She goes out of her way to consider the needs of other people and is sensitive to the burdens that other people carry. She has also been hopelessly unhappy for many years. She fights bouts of depression, extreme overeating, and hoarding phobias. She has been to I don't know how many qualified therapists and has been prescribed a bunch of different medications. Some of the meds work pretty well in keeping her balanced, but her unhappiness can overtake her to the point that she refuses to take anything. My heart breaks for her.

In the best of times, she looks to Richie as the complete source of her validation. Sadly, he is not an expressive guy, and though he has tried, he has not been able to relate to her need for affirmation. In the worst of times, their tranquil, loving household becomes a war zone, and howitzers of hurtful words have been thrown back and forth for so many years that their mutual wounds are deep and may never heal. Lynette has assumed that it is her fault that Richie does not "want" to validate her. She started out just feeling guilty about the things that she thought contributed to pushing him away. She must be "doing" something bad. The weight from giving birth that she didn't quite lose, her auburn hair versus being the blonde that she figures he *really* wants, and so on. Then even after losing the weight and getting countless makeovers, nothing changes. Guilt turned to shame. She is now not just doing something bad; she believes she *is* a bad person.

And then there's Marianne. She's a believer. We've also known her and her family for many years. Her husband, Gerard, is a personal trainer and started his own very successful fitness center. He attends church but has never talked much about a personal relationship with God. When I engaged him in a conversation about his salvation, he politely said he liked to "keep private matters private." Marianne chose to be an at-home mom. She would spend hours coming up with great meals and invite us over to hang out with them. The way her eyes gleamed when we all raved about how delicious the food was just about lit up the dining room. We were all good friends during that painful period when Gerard announced that after twenty-one years of marriage, he was leaving her for a "prettier" woman. OK, so maybe she did not, in fact, fit the cultural idea of beauty, but that kind of cruelty is inexcusable. The gut-wrenching process of breaking up what was such a wonderful family and now having her two boys and two girls split time with her and Gerard's new household was just about more than she could take. But it did not break her.

It's been almost eleven years now, and although Marianne has not found a new relationship, she has not lost the gleam. She has reordered her priorities and gone through the process of establishing a "new normal" for herself and her children. She makes sure that they never hear a critical word about their father because she understands how important it is for them to have a good dad in their lives. She has found some constructive outlets for her anger and disappointment by taking tai chi and doing a kickboxing class at the local YMCA!

What a contrast, right? The underlying issue is that Lynette has never been able to accept herself. Somewhere in the dark recesses of her mind and perhaps even her childhood, she came to believe that she was just not good enough. There is a powerful scripture found in the book of 1 John 3:20–21. It basically says that if your conscience doesn't condemn you, then you will find it easy to accept the truth of what God says about you. The corollary would then be that if the soundtrack in your mind tells you that you are no good or unworthy, you'll have a tough time agreeing with the good news of the gospel. So on the surface, Lynette would almost appear doomed, right? But if she is, it is only because she is not able to tape over that track and hear a new song. You see, the last part of that verse in 1 John 3 says that ultimately God's love and grace is more powerful than even our conscience. I'll never give up on Lynette because I know God never will.

Chapter Two

Developing Unconscious Competence

A Consistently Repeatable Thought Process

Now that we've laid the foundation, let's start to build further toward success. Having addressed the spiritual dimension, we now focus on creating the right mental framework. To say it another way, once you begin to believe correctly, you will almost automatically begin to reason correctly. Proverbs 23 talks about us becoming who we believe we are. This is essentially acting on the fruit of the unconditional acceptance we just finished delving into. Now, however, the issue is developing a simple set of skills that become embedded in your mental habits to the point that you do them without thinking that much about them. It's "unconscious competence," a technique that describes the adult learning process in many ways. Here's a simple example I always use in conveying this to people.

When I was a toddler, I had a fascination with cars—they were fast, loud, and shiny. At that age, I had absolutely no understanding of what a car was all about, but I wanted to drive one. You could say that I was "unconsciously incompetent." I didn't even know what I didn't know. When I was five or six, my dad would let me sit on his lap on a deserted country road early on a Saturday morning and let me "drive." Actually, it helped me realize I had a choice to make. I could either see over the dashboard or touch the pedals but not both. At least, though, I'm "*consciously* incompetent." I've learned some of what I need to master to drive. Finally, at sixteen, you get to take driver's education. (Being from West Virginia, my dad made sure I was a skilled driver by the time I was twelve, but that's another story!) So except for parallel parking, when you have to think about what you're doing, driving a car can be pretty easy. At this point, we're "consciously competent." As long as you recall your training, you can drive successfully.

So first of all, I am decidedly not a morning person. I have no idea what value one can derive from being fully awake at 5:00 a.m., plus I've been driving now for umpteen years. It is not uncommon for me to be on the road at 5:30 a.m., making my way around the DC beltway. It's also not uncommon for me to "wake up" behind the wheel suddenly and remember I'm driving. I've driven for so long I barely have to think about it at all, although you would undoubtedly, as a fellow beltway traveler, prefer that I was. The fact is that, in terms of driving, I have become "unconsciously competent." OK, OK, *I know* I should be more alert behind the wheel, but you at least get the analogy, right? Sheesh. There are some things that we must learn to do that become a consistently repeatable thought process that we do well and do *unconsciously*.

The failure of most other approaches to success is that they require you to always focus on the principles of their approach. Many of those principles are also outside of your normal habits. It sounds great when you are first trained in the techniques. You're absorbed in carrying out each step at a high level of concentration. When the training is over, you get back to your life and all its demands. You eventually lose focus and can no longer follow the steps you were so diligently practicing. A better approach is to create a way of *thinking about things* so that your actions will lead to success "unconsciously." Yes, you are correct. You still must master the way you think about things, but because this is done within the context of your current habits, you don't have to make a transition back to your regular life. The other advantage here is that this is not a formula that is applied to a narrow dimension such as becoming successful in your career, being a successful parent, or amassing wealth. The things we will consider *are* your life. The paltry amount of effort it takes to develop unconscious competence will amaze you, not to mention the powerful impact it will have on you, everyone you care about, and everything in your life. Let's talk about three areas where developing unconscious competence will greatly enrich your life and your walk with the Lord.

1. *Mindfulness*: developing a high level of awareness of how you affect people
2. *Resilience*: understanding and embracing the reality of change
3. *Decision-making*: consistently making the best-balanced choice when faced with options

Mindfulness

You can tell when someone doesn't have it even if you don't know what to call it. It's the glaringly obvious fact that someone you are interacting with or observing has no idea how they are coming across, affecting others, or being perceived by others. You watch them behave and realize they are not "mindful." Developing unconscious competence in this area can make or break every personal relationship you have.

Case Study: Wow, Dad!

I had the incredible pleasure of coaching youth soccer for a number of years. Our team won six or seven State championships and was less than thirty seconds away from going to the Nationals (nightmares still). Darius was an outstanding ten-year-old midfielder. The kid would give you his last breath and was easy to coach. His dad was a consistent supporter of the team but had never participated in sports himself as a kid. He was almost your stereotypical mild-mannered accountant and basic good guy—except when the whistle blew to start the match! His focus was totally on Darius and shouting instructions and "encouragement" to him from the stands on a nearly constant basis. He had never played, so his instructions were rarely on point, and what passed for encouragement was embarrassing. He turned into a raving near lunatic whenever Darius lost the ball, got beat by another player on the dribble, or missed putting the ball in the back of the net—none of these ever happening with any sort of regularity. I had several polite conversations with Dad about calming down and being more supportive. For a hardworking ten-year-old boy to be browbeaten to near tears by his dad in front of fans, teammates, and opponents just wasn't cool. And each time, he assured me that he was and wondered why I was singling him out.

On one occasion, we were playing a tournament in ninety-degree heat against a team from the Soviet Union. They were all fast and precise passers. Darius ran a total of about 150 yards up and down the field on one series of counterattacks by both teams, ending up missing a tackle, sprawled out in front of our fans. His dad flew out of the stands, screaming at him to get up and keep running. I had to ask him to leave the field, which of course didn't sit well at all. He eventually had to be restrained by the other parents. It was not the last time, and ultimately, Darius's Mom decided that playing soccer was not healthy for their family. To this day, Dad believes he was treated unfairly.

You have probably encountered versions of Darius's Dad at work, on a school committee, or even in your own family. They are everywhere. People lack the ability to display what is referred to as "emotional intelligence." They have little to no perception of how their behavior is affecting others. It is the single biggest reason, for example, that people can love their work and hate their job. Their boss, manager, or supervisor has too little emotional intelligence. There are numerous books written about the subject. It has been identified as a mandatory requirement for any position of leadership. For example, pretty much all the top business schools require a course in emotional intelligence to graduate.

Lack of emotional intelligence hurts any relationship. In fact, the closer the person is to you, the more your emotional intelligence matters. Think how much Darius's Dad is harming him and slowly destroying the bond with his son. Remember reading about Lynette earlier? Her husband, Richie, is another example of someone with too little display of emotional intelligence. He is totally blind to her need for affirmation from him and, therefore, unable to even begin to bridge the gap. He's not responsible for how she feels, of course. But he is responsible for how he affects her for good or ill. With more mindfulness, he'd know that as a husband, he has a responsibility to have a discussion with her about her needs and to help focus her away from dependence on him. The sad thing is that Richie loves Lynette just as Darius's dad loves him. But without a level of mindfulness, the love is lost.

There are books, videos, and seminars you can check out to get further into mindfulness and the full scope of emotional intelligence. I'm not saying they are not useful, but you can develop mindfulness at a level of unconscious competence fairly easily. Here's what it takes.

Do an honest inventory. Be honest with yourself regarding what emotion you are feeling that prompts your "best" and "worst" behavior.

Ask someone you trust (three or four people is even better) to give you some honest feedback on how you come across, how you are perceived, and what behaviors positively and negatively affect people when you are around them.

Pick the one least productive behavior that seems to be predominant or you hear as a common theme.

Commit to observing yourself in your interactions. When you see the behavior, remind yourself of what you saw.

That's it? Really? Yep, that's it. Once you ask yourself what emotion you are feeling, that prompts you to make a neurobiological connection that will gradually alter the behavior. (We'll talk more about neurobiology later.) Before you know it, you will develop unconscious competence. Now understand this—you will likely not be perfect. But even when you make a mistake, you'll know it. That will enable you, worst case, to fix it when situations go wrong.

How to Build Resilience

So here's the tough thing about life. Change is the most consistent aspect of existence and the most difficult thing to deal with. The more progress you can make toward dealing with this conundrum, the fuller, richer, and exciting your life will be.

The starting point for understanding resilience is appreciating how we are built as human beings. If you read Psalm 139, it will tell you about what an amazing creation we are. The intricacy and complexity with which we were designed is truly fascinating.

For example, we have a built-in set of biochemical responses that prepare us to deal with any threat, real or perceived, that enters our environment. In fact, one of our brain's primary jobs is to scan our environment multiple times each second to monitor the presence of any such threat. If it perceives danger, it will begin to release powerful chemicals throughout our system to prepare us to address it. These chemicals give us nearly supernatural strength as well as redirecting the flow of blood through our body so that our vital organs will be protected. Even some of the blood that circulates in the brain itself gets diverted so that your heart, liver, lungs, etc. are fully protected. This response occurs without our conscious mind even being aware of it. This is a very basic description. There is much more to it. But even with this basic understanding, you can draw a few important conclusions.

Your physical brain and your conscious mind are two different things. Therefore, your brain makes decisions for you initially without consulting your conscious mind. These decisions automatically establish the basis of your mental and emotional state.

Your neurobiological system works to keep your environment as stable as possible. In other words, it doesn't like change. Or more accurately, it perceives change as a threat and will resist the possibility, or even the thought, of something being different tomorrow from what it was yesterday.

I have found that most people are unaware of these aspects of our being. The consequence is that when change does occur, they are unequipped to bring themselves to a place of balance. They struggle emotionally and feel as if they are on a never-ending roller coaster. They have incredible difficulties in this regard—fits of anger and rage, uncertainty and mental paralysis, even the risk of varying degrees of depression. And this is not even the biggest problem.

The biggest problem is that they give in to that neurobiological pressure to keep things the same—*even when they are unhappy with the way things are.* This is an incredible tragedy both in the sense of everyday life and in one's spiritual development as well.

Case Study: Stuck

Ron is one of the most faithful guys you will ever meet. If he says he will do it, he'll do it. If for some reason he falls short, he will 'fess up right away and make it good. Ron went into the military right after finishing high school in Dallas, Texas. (He's a proud Texan by the way!). In the military, he obtained certifications in computer science, information security, and cybersecurity. Ask him anything about a computer or data systems, and he can tell you more than you'd want to know! He has kept up with the vast changes in technology and is current on the latest developments. After his stint was over, he settled up north and took a job in the state government agency that oversees government buildings, vehicles, and other equipment. Shortly afterward, he met Caitlyn, and they got married. Ron has been in that same position since I met him thirty-six years ago. He has yet to receive a promotion but has gotten the normal step increases in his salary. For at least the last twenty-five years, he has been bored stiff. For the last fifteen, he has been downright unhappy and began to drink heavily. He was so unhappy and bored ten years ago that he says it was the reason he had an affair with a woman who works in another agency that shares the same building. Although he and Caitlyn have stayed together, not much trust or joy has been restored to their marriage. I've lost count of the number of conversations I have had with him over the years, encouraging him to see what other jobs, careers, vocations, or educational opportunities there might be for him. He is always receptive and says he will consider it, only to eventually return to the stream of complaints about how bad things are in his life. Ron was stuck. Five years ago, I agreed to go with him to his first Alcoholics Anonymous (AA) meeting. In just his third meeting, something miraculous happened. The speaker apparently talked about this neurobiological stuff I just mentioned. She went through the grief adjustment process first put forth by the Swiss psychiatrist Dr. Elisabeth Kübler-Ross in the early 1970s. The simple stages people go through when they face traumatic change are denial, anger, bargaining, depression, and eventually, acceptance. When our idea of normal is disrupted, our brain takes us through an almost predictable process of establishing a new normal. Ron, however, discovered something a bit different but related. He realized that he was so afraid of change that he felt more secure doing something he hated rather than risking a move into the unknown. He realized he had been depressed for years and years. It was that sense of sadness and loss that caused such a faithful person to be unfaithful to a loving wife, not to mention violating his own dignity by becoming an alcoholic. Understanding how we are built and how we react to change was, to put it mildly, an unbelievable eye-opener. Within two months after incorporating these insights, he lost the desire to drink. Within nine months, Ron was working for the State Office of Emergency Management. (He is in a leadership-development cohort, being groomed for a management position down the road.) He and Caitlyn still have a way to go in rebuilding their marriage, but when you see them together, you can tell that "faithful Ron" may well have performed the sometimes-impossible feat of renewing the broken trust.

What saved Ron's life was becoming aware of his unwillingness to embrace change. Knowing the natural responses that human beings must go through can save your life as well. That level of self-awareness also goes along with the ideas of mindfulness and emotional intelligence that we talked about. But there's more to this than just knowing.

What is an even more valuable lesson for you is the importance of staying *ahead* of the need for change. Yes, it's great to know how to deal with change so that you get through it, no doubt. Resilience is defined as the ability to bounce back when life hits hard. But why spend your life getting good at getting through stuff or just bouncing back? Why not seek it out yourself and reap the benefits at a higher and deeper level? In fact, the most resilient people stay aware of the necessity to prepare for change on an incremental basis. They are always aware that things are changing. Rather than wait for a disruptive event, they look for small ways to make adjustments:

They are always learning. They read books on new topics.

They take classes to enlarge their base of experience.

They travel to places they have never been even if they are close by.

They try different food.

You name it.

These folks easily and effortlessly build their resilience by practicing change. The marvelous by-product is that when things get tough, they are better prepared to find that "new normal." Better yet, life is always exciting because there will be always be something new to see, to do, and of course, to eat!

And it gets even better. If you are a believer, you had best adopt this same attitude to your spiritual life. The reason I believe we have so many denominations and so many congregations full of unhappy people in those congregations is that they are no longer growing. They have camped out around a very limited understanding of God and an even more limited understanding of how Jesus is living His life through them. The Bible makes it clear that we are to be constantly growing up into the fullness of the reality of Christ within us. The vast majority of Christians, if I may be so bold, have unconsciously allowed their neurobiological impulses to keep everything the same to infiltrate their relationship with God. They are protecting what they have always known and always thought to the point that they resist growing in the knowledge of God. You would be shocked to see the number of New Testament verses that suggest you should be doing exactly the opposite.

Once again, I'll avoid inundating you with that list and encourage you to do your own homework. It will bless you, I promise. And I do get it. It is a little scary to expose your traditional beliefs to the possibility of having to unlearn some things. But what if those traditional beliefs limit your opportunity for a greater depth of relationship with the Lord? And as we've already talked about, there's a good chance as well that some of those traditional beliefs are wrong. If either is true, then you owe it yourself, and those you care about, to grow. The Lord has so much more in store for us than we can see. Ephesians 3:20 says in so many words that the good things the Lord wants to have happened in your life are so much better than anything you could dream up. Step out of the boat. Decide to embrace a little change every time you go to read the Bible, every time you sing some praise, and every time you pray. We'll come full circle on this point at the conclusion of this book.

Decisions, Decisions, Decisions

So speaking of having to decide, making good decisions may be the single most important skill that a person can have. Decisions have futurity. In other words, when you make a decision, the impact usually occurs somewhere down the road. Being able to have confidence that you made the best choice at the time you make the decision is the key to ensuring that those longer-term impacts are, at best, beneficial in creating your future reality and, at worst, minimize the negative aspects. Sadly, we do not generally teach people how to make decisions. And you and I both have seen far too many acquaintances, friends, and loved ones suffer the consequences of bad decisions, not to mention the ones we've had to live through personally.

Decision-making needs to become part of your unconscious competence. You need a dependable, repeatable process that can handle the full range of life's issues. Most people are successful because they made a few right decisions. As a believer, your having the Holy Spirit as your teacher and guide gives a phenomenal advantage. You have to know how to use it, though. You should be aware that the Lord is directing your path and that you only need to follow that path. This begins by submitting the direction of your life to the Lord's will.

Psalm 37:4 lets us know that if we commit our direction to the Lord, then we can be assured that our purpose will be established. Simply put, the Lord will make sure we are heading in the right direction. Proverbs 16:3, in turn, tells us that if we commit the things that we decide to do to the Lord, then we can be assured that your thought process will become aligned with the Lord's will. This is such incredibly great news! It takes away such a significant amount of stress that we usually experience in figuring things out. The starting place for both scriptures, you will notice, is to "commit." It has been painful over the years to see how the traditional church, some televangelists, and other so-called ministries have made this so difficult for people. There are books and DVDs that sell you formulas, conferences you need to attend to "get under the anointing," and on and on. It's painful because it is so much simpler and easier to execute the idea of commitment. All it takes is a simple prayer that is prayed with sincere focus and that comes from a calm and quieted heart.

Before you embark on any venture, enter any agreement, or take any step in an important direction, get yourself calmed and quieted.

Ask the Lord to guide and direct you.

Then *believe* that you will be guided and directed.

Return to that calm and quiet place periodically, and check in with the Lord.

A part of me would like for this to be a bit more complex. It would make me seem more intelligent, I'm thinking. For the sake of this book and my interest in you being successful, I'm thrilled that it is this easy. Following this pattern as a way of life will guarantee that you will never be far from the center of the Lord's will. And even when you find yourself on the perimeter of that will, you can rely on the Lord's love and grace to gently ease you back toward the center—for the most part, without you having to do much at all. We are called "colaborers" by God in 1 Corinthians 3. It means that we have a small role to play in the work that gets done. When it comes to decisions, there are a few specific things we need to get clear in our minds to know we are taking the right course of action:

The Goal: We are called upon, I believe, to ensure that what we are attempting to accomplish is consistent with the direction we have been provided. The goal of the decision has to be clear to you. Sometimes writing the goal down using the fewest words possible is helpful. A concise statement will also be valuable throughout the decision process as a way of keeping you aligned.

Constraints: Most decisions are bound by some important restrictions, limitations, or other boundaries. These may be time, money, or other parameters. The issue here is that we absolutely must avoid choosing options that violate those boundaries. If we do, we will have immediately made a bad decision. There are usually only a precious few constraints in a decision situation. Knowing and adhering to them, however, is paramount to protecting yourself from making absolutely the wrong choice.

Objectives: Decisions are less about choosing a particular option and more about satisfying the needs or demands of a given situation. Objectives express those needs or demands. We are called upon to stay true to the objectives of the decision situation and not to be swayed by the allure or attractiveness of various options that come our way. Doing so is paramount to making the best choice. Decisions are all about satisfaction.

Information: The best option is the one that does the best overall job of meeting our objectives. While it is often hard to find an option that meets all of them, we are looking for the one that does the best overall job—giving you the most of what is important to you and the least of what you want to avoid. To make this work, you need to have some data on how each option satisfies each objective. The more that is at stake in the decision, the fuller and more detailed the data needs to be. Yes, there is a place for our emotions in decision-making, but not at this point. This is where using the analytical faculties that God has given you need to be employed.

Risk assessment: Once you know which option does the best job of meeting the objectives, you will want to think about any inherent risk if you were to go with that choice. This is completely different from constraints. Risk assessment uncovers things that could go wrong when the decision is implemented. This is where things so often fall apart, and no one can see why it happened. Lots of decisions look great at the moment. But implementation risks are often outside the decision framework! If future conditions reduce the chance of receiving the benefits, then it may be better to go with the second-best option if its risk is substantially less. Again, decisions are less about choosing a particular option and more about satisfying the needs or demands of a given situation. Assess the risk before you go with the top choice.

Case Study: College-Bound Collette

Collette is one of the brightest twenty-year-old kids you'll ever meet. Her intelligence is only exceeded by her sweet disposition, humility, and generous soul. She has always been one of those "college-bound" students. Her school guidance counselors had helped her determine early on that a larger school was a better fit for her. Collette also felt that a diversity of students in terms of their career interests would be even more motivating and stretch her intellectual capabilities. In addition to her intelligence, she is an awesome artist, in terms of performance and creativity. She had the lead in the school play three years running, and her paintings have had the honor of being displayed in a small gallery in her community. Since she was in junior high, she has wanted to be a museum curator. She did an internship in the last two summers and fell in love with the idea. Her parents fully support her direction. Her mom, Enid, is a university professor in biology, and her dad, Carl, owns a very popular auto mechanic shop.

A curator not only has to know about art but also should have a well-rounded skill set. They should be able to manage complex projects and develop, present, and communicate messages through design. Curators, at the highest levels, have great writing and presentation skills and are adept at managing fund-raising campaigns and cultivating donors. In larger museums, they also need to be conversant with the ins and outs of information technology and high-level database management. When it came time for choosing colleges to apply to, Collette was heavily pursued by the top art schools in the country—Rhode Island School of Design, Cranbrook Academy of Art (Michigan), Bard College, the Art Institute of Chicago, Maryland Institute College of Art, Hunter College (New York), and the list goes on. Her parents were ecstatic at the opportunities. They were even more excited when the top three schools gave her nearly full scholarships. Much to their shock, not only was Collette unfazed by the attention of the art schools, but the list of schools she had decided to apply to had none of her suitors on it! Her list included Johns Hopkins, George Washington, Syracuse, Tufts, and the University of Washington in Seattle. The typically peaceful household that Collette and her parents had always enjoyed was significantly disrupted. Much to their credit, her parents keep a reasonable degree of calm, relying on her track record of making intelligent choices. But they were upset enough that every attempt to have a reasoned discussion failed, taking its toll on all three of them. When enough dust finally settled, they convinced Collette to allow me to facilitate a conversation.

I have to tell you, as a parent, that I was subconsciously thinking of ways to steer Collette back toward one of the art schools, knowing what I thought I knew. Consciously—and fortunately—I had determined to play the role I was asked to as a facilitator. Good decision on my part! You see, Collette had a process. Given that her goal was to be a museum curator, this required an advanced degree. Her focus was less on the college and more on the quality of the graduate program. The graduate program would provide that broad range of skills beyond just an aptitude for art. While the art schools had good programs, their interest in Collette was at the undergraduate level and in furthering her performance and painting skills. In each case, her chosen schools would also potentially offer her a five-year program accelerating her master's degree. Given that her guidance counselors had helped her determine that a large school with diverse student interests was the best direction, all the art schools were at the other end of the spectrum. After hearing such a well-thought-out decision process, Collette's parents wholeheartedly consented to her list of schools. Of course, she was accepted into all of them. Her top two choices both offered her full scholarships. She will be entering her senior year and has already been offered a position in the third largest museum in the country.

Not every decision dilemma ends this well, of course. I could share with you ten examples of how the lack of clarity in the decision process has caused people to buy the wrong car, buy the wrong house, or accept the wrong job. Did the Lord let them go astray? Certainly not. In most cases, their emotions got in the way, or they overlooked the need for data to back up what they thought they heard in prayer. Had they aligned themselves and stayed with that alignment by getting clear on the decision, the results would have been different. But here again, this is why God's love and grace are so instrumental. Even when we make mistakes or miss it, the Lord takes our blunders and uses them to open us up to deeper realms of spiritual insights.

Chapter Three

Living by Revelation

So let's talk about those deeper realms. To avoid that tendency to make this seem difficult, let me assure you that the difference between the simple spiritual insights and these deeper realms is simply time. While we are all different and have different spiritual capacities, depth comes with experience. Salvation is intended to be an effortless long-distance run, not a frenetic, exhausting hundred-yard dash. Our current culture does not lend itself to these realities. If you are a young person, let's say in your twenties or early thirties, you'll appreciate getting a glimpse into these aspects if you haven't already begun to plummet these depths. We'll talk about the following:

1. Understanding what "faith" is and how yours increases
2. Identifying how to now act on your purpose
3. Learning how to live from the "inside out"

Having Faith

The idea of faith has been greatly misconstrued in the traditional church setting. On top of that, too many televangelists have taken advantage of people by merchandising the concept. (Let me say that there are many more honest and legitimate ministers out there and that giving money to support their efforts is a good thing. You just should know the difference between them and the illegitimate ones that prey on human frailty.) You have likely heard others scare you by citing that you can't please God if you don't have faith and on and on. Faith is essential to your relationship with the Lord. There is no dispute over that. The problem is in having a clear biblical understanding of what it is and how it functions. I'll address this by first talking about what biblical faith is *not*.

Biblical faith is not the following:

- Blind. We are told in the Letter to the Hebrews that faith is substance and evidence. It is evidence of what is not seen, but it is not blind. That twisting of the truth has shipwrecked so many people's lives.

- Deciding what you want and applying a formula to ensure that God agrees with you and acts in your request. The Lord does honor the things that you want. But it is foolish, immature, and irreverent to try to manipulate faith solely to get what you want.

- Hoping that the Lord notices your need and does something about it. The underlying supposition misses the reality of who and what God is. The Lord not only knew that you would have a need but already made provision for your need to be met. The underlying supposition places you in the position of a beggar rather than a son or daughter.

- An emotional state. The same Letter to the Hebrews assures us that Jesus, through the Holy Spirit, has intimate compassion for how you feel. Your emotional state matters to the Lord. It's just that your emotions are not generally a credible indicator of reality.

OK, so what *is* faith? The word used for *faith* in the New Testament is best translated as "to be persuaded." So how are you persuaded of something? If a salesperson knocked on your door to sell you a product, he or she would make the best effort to persuade you to buy. You'd rarely just accept verbal claims about the product. You would probably want either a demonstration of the product's attributes right there in front of you or at least be provided with a list of references of others who could testify that the product did what the salesperson said it would do. And suppose he or she proved to you that the product worked, you bought it, and had a long period of satisfying results. By chance, the same salesperson shows up again and has yet another product to offer to you. While you would still want *some* evidence, it would be decidedly less because he or she has established some credibility with you. You could even say that you have developed a certain level of trust. And suppose this same scenario repeats itself year after year after year. Now, as a wise consumer, you would hardly ever buy anything sight unseen, but this salesperson's credibility would continue to grow and grow. At some point, you could even say that you have "faith" in them. They have established a track record of performing in the manner that now causes you to believe what they say. Simple, right? Biblical faith is simply being persuaded that God will do what has been promised because a track record of "credibility" has been established. This track record can come from promises received in the written word (the New Testament uses the word *logos* for this) or promises that may have been received in your heart during a time of prayer (the New Testament uses the word *rhema* for this).

Study Challenge:

In chapter 11 of the Letter To the Hebrews, look at the list of the names of Bible figures who are cited for their faith. Read about their relationship with the Lord, and

> you will see that their faith was not "blind." It developed by the Lord establishing a track record of faithfulness in honoring what had been spoken to them. They were thus persuaded.

I think you can see the implications for having a correct versus incorrect understanding of biblical faith. It provides an anchor for basically everything you do and how you handle everything that comes your way.

Case Study: My Darkest Days

Right when I was ordained as a pastor, I remember sensing the Holy Spirit tell me that I was going to encounter a significant trial. Like most of us, I imagine, I did my best to figure out what type of trial it was going to be. Knowing how demanding ministry can be, I figured it was connected to the demands of leading a congregation and didn't give it much thought. Three months later, I was diagnosed with "cause unknown" kidney disease. Despite efforts to reverse the process, my kidney function fell below the required levels to cleanse my system of deadly toxins. I had to undergo dialysis and went through the protocols to be placed on a transplant list. If you're not familiar with what dialysis is all about, you're lucky. For four hours, three to four times a week, you get hooked up to a machine that takes your blood, runs it through a cleansing process, and returns it to your body. You have to eventually have a tube surgically inserted, often into your arm, for the procedure to be done. Prior to that surgery, a tube is immediately (with no anesthesia, I might add) put into your neck or into your chest cavity. Your food and water intake is substantially altered as the accumulation of fluid, salt, and potassium can be deadly. It works against your heart since, as the machine is attempting to pull the blood from your body, your heart is straining to hold on to it. I'm not going to walk you through all the horrors of the ordeal. But over the five years that I had to deal with dialysis, there were a *lot* of horrors. For example, occasionally, the settings on the machine cause your blood pressure to drop in an instant. It feels kind of like what I imagine it feels like to fall from the top of the Sears Tower. The tube in your arm can get blocked, and it has to be cleared by surgery. I had nine of those. And on and on.

I really did try to "man up" initially, but I have to tell you, it got to me. I hated getting up at 4:30 a.m., getting strapped into that chair, and managing my anxiety for essentially five hours. I hated it. Worst of all, I could not figure out why God would let this happen to me. I had "given up" everything to follow Jesus. I altered my career plan and agreed to pastor the congregation. Why would God allow this to happen to *me*? The more I sank into pity and despair, the more the cushy recliner I sat in to have dialysis began to seem like an electric chair. And three times a week, I walked that "Green Mile" to my execution. The breaking point was traumatic. I told God one day, "Hey, I just don't care anymore. Do whatever you want to me. I'm done." There was more to come, though. Dialysis patients get to know each other quickly. We have lost most of our pride at this point in our lives and nearly all our pretense. We quickly form a tight-knit group trying to survive. At my Monday dialysis session, the always optimistic woman sitting in the chair to the right of me had a heart attack and died in the chair. At the Friday session, my older colleague who told the best stories of his childhood in Kentucky, as he sat in the chair to the left of me, did the same. Shaken is a mild term for how I was feeling.

Later that day, I got a call from a fellow pastor who told me that a minister friend of hers was in town, and would I be interested in getting my congregation together with hers at 7:00 p.m. for an impromptu meeting? His name was Sam Greene from Narrow Way Ministries in Jacksonville, Florida. Rita thought it was a good idea, and despite my total lack of spiritual energy, I agreed. I have learned to trust my wife's insight into these things. Because of it being a last-minute endeavor, I barely had time to meet the guy, and the service began. Sam led the praise—beautiful voice, skilled guitarist. He taught on Abraham believing God—solid message. And then he started to share prophetic words with members of our congregation. Now I knew these people, and I knew the situations and issues that they were facing. And I knew for a fact that he didn't know anything. I was listening with utter amazement as he encouraged them in precisely the areas where I knew they needed encouragement. And then he turned to me.

"Pastor, I hear the Lord confirming to you that you will live and not die." That was it. (I'm assuming here that you're aware that Sam had no knowledge of anything about me, being on dialysis to begin with and watching two other people I knew very well die in front of me just that week.) Almost immediately, I made the connection. That "trial" that I heard about years earlier? This was it. And because the Lord had already told me about it, and because it was just confirmed to me that I would survive, my heart revived within me in an instant. The following Monday, as I approached the dialysis chair, it looked different. Yes, it was no longer a place of execution. It was now a seat of mercy. It was the place I went to have my

> life saved. A year or so later, I was called to come into the hospital for a transplant. I have been functioning with little to no difficulties (not even the normal ones that people usually encounter) now going on twenty years.

As hopefully inspiring as this faith story may be, there are more than a few perversions of faith that you need to be on guard against.

Watch out for the "name it and claim it" folks. They want to reduce your notion of spiritual prosperity down to your ability to acquire material possessions. The subtle and, sometimes sadly, overt message is that the depth of your faith and spirituality is reflected in how much stuff you have been blessed with. People who don't have lots of stuff don't have faith. This is an incredible insult to millions of believers. I have ministered to the abysmally poor in places like Haiti and parts of Africa. They have little in the way of stuff, but their "faith"—the degree to which they are persuaded that the Lord will keep the promises made to them— would put the prosperity people to shame.

Watch out for the extreme "word of faith" folks. I say extreme because not all who consider themselves in this vein are off base. The ones to be concerned about are those who position your faith as a commodity that must be developed and grown so that it will work. This is similar to "name it and claim it." The distinction is that the creative power of your words can manipulate the will of the Lord and have things happen because you want them, not because it is the wisdom of the Lord. For example, many of the extreme folks will denigrate people who go to a doctor or take medicine for an illness versus just having faith. In fact, for them, the reason that you are sick to begin with is that you have no faith. The Lord heals people in all kinds of ways—with doctors and hospitals, with meds and without. You need to hear what the Lord's direction is for you rather than just deciding what it should be.

Watch out for the folks who make everything spiritual. What I mean by this is that those who use their faith to "spiritualize" things that don't go the way they thought they would. This is the other end of the spectrum from the first two. You're late for work so many times that you get fired. Your response is "The Lord was just ready for me to move on to an even better job!" You're on your way to an interview for a new job, and you run out of gas and miss it. Your response is "The devil just doesn't want me to have this job." Everything certainly is driven by the spiritual realm. We'll get into that shortly. But when we use the spiritual realm as an excuse for our shortcomings or failures, then we are perverting the idea of faith.

Watch out for anyone promoting a movement of God. I know I'll get into trouble on this one for sure, but truth is truth. Because most of the church's theology is based on the supposition that God is mad at us, most believers are waiting for the Lord to do something in the future to address their needs and issues. For these future events to occur, God logically has to do something different, hence the advent of a "new move of God." The vivid message of the gospel is that the Lord has already done everything that we need to be done.

Bible Study Challenge:

Read Ephesians, Colossians, Hebrews, 1 and 2 Peter, etc. You will see the word hath used to refer to the work of the Lord in us. Yes, we do step into deeper levels of understanding. But I hope you can easily see that waiting for God to do something that has already been done is nuts.

More concerning is that this theology has absolutely paralyzed believers. People are not stepping out and using the gifts and spiritual power that the Lord gave them in their salvation. They are still waiting to get it before they embark on changing the world around them by demonstrating the love of God. The New Testament is especially vigilant about us as believers stepping into the ministry we have been given.

Living on Purpose

What ministry? I could hear most of you ask yourselves that question. Boy, have we got a lot to talk about now. Not only has the traditional church's future-oriented theology paralyzed believers, our entire approach to ministry has done far worse. Remember Constantine? Well, ever since that time, the church has constructed an artificial and unbiblical separation between "ministers" and the people in the congregation. A biblical church structure has elders and deacons overseeing the congregation. Today church leaders are consumed with titles, prestige, and undue deference to their role in the body of Christ. As a pastor, I certainly agree that we should respect the leaders, but for heaven's sake, do we have to put them on pedestals and bow down to the greater level of spirituality that they absolutely *do not* possess? Radical as they may seem, it can be backed up by the Bible itself. You will not find a single time when *apostle, prophet, evangelist, pastor,* or *teacher* is capitalized and used as a title. These are functions, roles—honorable ones, yes, but it doesn't make some people better than the rest. Too many of our churches, I'm surmising, are filled with spectators who came to watch and support the ministry of the folks with a title. No wonder people are exiting in droves. They have actually read the Bible.

So what does the Bible say about this matter? For one, it says that the role of apostles, prophets, evangelists, and pastors (who are all viewed as teachers) is to help develop the ministries and the spiritual gifts of the rest of the congregation. This enables them to go out and, in turn, be effective ministers to their coworkers, colleagues, friends, family, and neighbors who need to know about God's love for them. This is how the body of Christ works.

Study Challenge:

Dissect Ephesians Chapter 4, especially verse 11–14. Determine what it says to you about what someone with a specific, named function should be focused on.

You'll see the flip side of this same idea in 1 Corinthians 5, that the purpose of your salvation was to make you a new creation in Christ so that you could fulfill your personal ministry of showing your coworkers, colleagues, friends, family, and neighbors how Jesus has already reconciled them back to God. Christ has restored to them the reality of their innocence. Again God is not mad at them. If they want to insist that, at some point, God was mad, then as a minister, your role is to let them know that, if that were true, the anger was expended on Jesus, and there is no anger left. I wish it were more complicated, but it just isn't. The sooner you see yourself as every bit a minister as those of us to do it more formally, the sooner you will begin to step into the richness of your purpose.

A key to stepping into it is discerning the focus of your purpose. The more singular the focus, the better. This is seen even more vividly in the business world. You may already be aware that most good ideas that the world stumbles upon are biblical principles implemented through spiritual truth. I have worked as a management consultant and facilitated a client's efforts in branding. Branding is a process for uncovering a unique identity that can be used to attract and hold on to customers. It is what organizations want to become known for on both a conscious and unconscious level. Successful ones know how to promote and deliver on their brand. For example, why do people stand in line for hours to get the latest iPhone? Because Apple has branded themselves as the provider of the latest and most cutting-edge technology. Why do folks pay three to five dollars for a cup of coffee in Starbucks? Because Starbucks has branded coffee as not just something to drink but an "experience" to participate in. Google has made themselves a part of our language. Even if you use a different search engine, you're still "googling." These are great examples of entities that know how to promote and deliver on a brand. On the other end are folks like Xerox. They are still a decent company but not the market leader in a business they "created." Even when you use an HP or a Canon to make a copy, you still plan to "xerox" it.

The wisdom here is to execute your purpose by, in so many words, discerning your unique "brand." so to speak. What is it, and how is it, that the Holy Spirit seems to express itself through you? Keep in mind that this unique brand wants to express itself in any situation or capacity you find yourself operating in, whether it's at work, in your family, or among your friends. It will be the basis for reading the purpose in the situations you find yourself in. It will be the reason why the Lord may have had you there. Doing some introspection and answering a few simple questions like these is all it takes to begin to develop this "personal brand":

What recurring themes can you observe over the course of your life? You will discover that you likely have found yourself in similar situations on a regular basis. These situations contain the needs and issues that your gift is intended to address. You could also include here any encouragements, prophetic words, etc. that have been given to you that seem to reinforce these themes.

What specific principles or values are most important to you? The things that you care deeply about will typically form the basis of your character. Your gifts are the channel through which that character will minister to others.

Where do you draw your energy from, and what things excite and motivate you? Although the Lord specializes in working through our weaknesses, that does not mean that power will not flow through the talents that already seem to be demonstrated through your life.

What do other people say they see in you? This is further down on the list for sure, but consider the observations of people whose objectivity and lack of motive can be relied upon.

Case Study: Who, Me?

Lydia is one of the most well-traveled people I know. She was born in Belize in Central America, in the town of Lord's Bank, about thirty minutes from Belize, City.

She moved to Alberta, Canada, when she was ten and went to college in Texas, where she met Kendall, her husband-to-be, who was in the Air Force. By the time we met Lydia, she had lived in sixteen different countries. You would think that she was an actual princess or at least came from some type of royalty. She has this air of graciousness and gracefulness about her. She is a marvelous conversationalist, and although she's an introvert, strangers make her face light up, and she launches herself easily in building a genuine rapport with anyone. Her gift for putting on any event, from the simplest to the most formal, makes Martha Stewart seem like a neophyte. Every—and I mean every—detail gets covered. Her skill at taking inexpensive items and turning them into elaborate-looking fixtures is pure genius.

Although she wants to do things her way, she is never condescending, pushy, or the slightest bit arrogant. In fact, you might even say she is a bit timid, especially when it comes to spiritual things. Given she has endured and triumphed in so many areas—overcoming cancer, for example—she lacked confidence in her ability to act out her salvation. Whenever we would talk about her capacity for ministry, her response was some version of "But what can I do? I don't have any particular spiritual gifts or ability." The emphasis of our ministry as pastors has always been the idea of equipping other people for the ministry the Lord has given them. Rita and I have tried in earnest to take the Ephesians 4:11–12 instructions seriously. We sat down with Lydia and led her through a similar set of questions. It seems that "hospitality" was a recurring theme in her life. She told us about how her parents, who were not believers, routinely invited people who needed a place to stay to board up with them as long as they needed. Her mom was one of the ultracompassionate people and one of the best cooks in Lord's Bank. Whenever there were leftovers, she would call down the street, letting anyone in earshot know that there was food available. When Lydia was in college, she found herself being prevailed upon by everyone on the dorm floor to cook up a pot of "stew chicken" or rice and beans. She joked that they bought the pot, the food, and all the ingredients if she would do the honors. Everyone loves her food.

Coincidentally, she confessed she loves talking to people, especially strangers, and feels fulfilled when she is taking care of others. You can probably see where this is going, can't you? Well, Lydia certainly did, and now her ministry is extending hospitality to people in any way and whenever she can. And of course, with the recognition of her "personal brand," the Lord just keeps sending people her way to be touched by her unique gift of imparting God's love. People are probably more touched by the gospel of Lydia's hospitality than any sermon they will ever hear. Her next goal is to create a "hospitality blog" and share her ideas with an even broader audience.

Now that, my friends, is a real ministry. Of course, you may not hear that kind of gift touted alongside the folks that lead a congregation or have a title. But if you read what the Book says and not what someone tries to make you believe what it says, then your definition of biblical ministry will change.

"Honey, That's Stupid"

Those who grasp the reality of the gospel begin to change not only their definition of ministry but also the way they see their purpose being carried out. They begin to understand that they are living the life of God from the inside out and not from the outside in. How can I make this plainer? Those who grasp the gospel are less affected by what they *see* happening and more by the deep spiritual principles that they understand are guiding and directing those external events. Our natural environment is limited by the laws that govern the operation of time, space, and matter. Those laws generally create predictable outcomes because of the finite boundaries within which they are enclosed. The "spiritual realm" exists outside those boundaries of time and space and is therefore not subject to its limitations. (I know this may sound like new-age nonsense to some of you, but that may be because you have never read much about quantum mechanics or quantum physics. I'd recommend you do some googling on the topic. You'll see that scientists, with no biblical agenda, are realizing there are properties around us that violate the traditional laws of physics.)

What you'll begin to appreciate is that the "spiritual realm" often operates exactly the opposite of the way the "natural" world does. For example, think of the principle of giving. The Bible encourages you to "give it away" and more will be produced in its place. The Bible insists that forgiving, and relinquishing your right to revenge, is the way to ensure personal justice. It even goes so far as to say that if you bless the people who intend to do the most harm to you, your blessings will flow in abundance. Wacky, under the principles of our natural realm. This idea of "living by revelation" will be the key to success with your family, your career, and anything else to put your hands to. Let's just look at one example of this.

You probably grew up hearing that opposites attract. As you got older, it seemed to make less sense because opposites didn't seem to get along so well. The problem is that the idea of diversity is fundamental to everything that happens on the planet. At the atomic level, it's the tension between negative, positive, and uncharged particles, with quarks and gluons binding things together. The real value of this may be, the more you experienced the inconvenient conflict of dealing with people who were different than you, the more you were motivated to surround yourself with people like you. It's comfortable and easy. And it's deadly. The inability to embrace heterogeneity in any of its forms is a death knell to your success in any venue. Unsure about this? If you work in any type of organization, you see the failure to handle diversity crippling your ability to move ahead. In the staff meeting, diverse perspectives are rarely tolerated. Any new idea is greeted with an immediate "We tried that before" or "It will never work." The group mentality enforces sameness, homogeneity, and reinventing the wheel. Conflicts between employees degenerate into childish complaints about differences in work styles, communication styles, and personal preferences. And the boss is so ill-equipped to address these issues that he or she turns a blind eye and a deaf ear. Is that close to your experience?

If not, try this on for size. You had this very specific list of requirements for a mate or companion. Lo and behold, the person you are attracted to and that seems to be attracted to you is doing all the right things during the whole time you are dating. You decide to marry, and about six months into the deal, something seems to have gone amiss. You discover that, in fact, along a broad spectrum of issues, the two of you couldn't be more different. Every conversation has a tone of stress to it because you just don't seem even to be speaking the same language. Worst case, this gulf leads to a divorce and dissolution of a family.

The spiritual truth that underpins these and many other circumstances is that diversity is where the real strength lies. It's just that too few people know that. At work or in an intimate relationship, they are expecting something else. If all people think the same way, they make the same mistakes. If you get that, then you'll expect to hear a different viewpoint in the staff meeting. You'll value your mate because you know you're not smart enough to figure it all out on your own. The other person's varying perspective becomes the saving grace.

Rita and I have been together for over forty years. I mentioned earlier that I have been in business for a while. Over the years, I have come up with untold numbers of ideas and business ventures, which I share with her so we can decide whether to invest. Her normal response is "Honey, that's stupid." Understand that she says it in a nice way with no intent to offend. She's just honest. However, nice or not, "Honey, that's stupid" is not my first choice of responses. I want to hear "Honey, you've done it again. What a brilliant idea." It's not easy listening to that divergent point of view. But you must ask yourself an even more important question. If she *had* gone along with my ideas over the years, what do you think the state of our finances might be? Yep, the word *homeless* comes to mind! When I ask her a question, I've learned not to need confirmation that I am right. I'm hoping she can help me avoid being wrong. No, it does not come automatically. I'm not suggesting that it doesn't take some effort and a huge dose of humility. I AM saying that it is essential to being successful. And yes, there are some core areas where we agree totally. We'll revisit this dynamic when we talk about marriage in just a bit.

In your relationship with God, the benefits of understanding just this one principle are even more profound. In the Book of Romans, chapter 8 tells us that the various circumstances in the lives of believers are producing "synergy" for those who have insight into their purpose. *Synergy* is a Greek word that means when you put things together, you will often experience an outcome that could not have been predicted by merely looking at the combination of those things. Something unexpected occurs because of the interaction of unobvious properties of the things being combined. And the more different the combined elements are, the more dynamic the synergistic effect. When the folks at work can incorporate the divergent thinking of their colleagues, what they can achieve for the organization will exceed the combined value of their individual thinking. When I can listen to Rita's reaction to my ideas, what we can then accomplish will end up being unpredictably better than our individual capabilities combined. When you being to apply this type of revelation to the practical aspects of your life, the results you can achieve will be unpredictable as well.

Chapter Four

Practical Application

Everything that we have talked about comes together in the application of your salvation to the core activities of your life. If the value of being a child of God is relegated to your attendance at church, then you've missed the boat, as they say. It is the Lord's intent to establish the kingdom in everything that matters to you. Put it this way—rather than have you focus on making your future home in heaven, the Lord wants you to bring heaven into your home now. Of course, there are trials and tribulations in life. But there's a huge difference between the mindset of most people—unfortunately even many believers—and what is readily available to you through the power of the gospel. You see, some people experience peace and wholeness as periodic mini-vacations from the consistent level of chaos and stress that characterizes their daily life. God's design is that your salvation establishes for you a consistent level of peace and wholeness, periodically and minimally interrupted by the chaos and stress around you.

So let's round this all out and see how the gospel affects these core areas and activities:

Covenant and Sex. We'll get this discussion out of the way first, mainly because once we lay out the underlying principles, the rest of the discussion will flow easily.

Love and Marriage. This will be the shortest marriage manual you have ever seen, but hopefully, we can capture the core of what it takes to live happily ever after. We'll touch upon being single as well.

Parenting. The Bible indicates that the main reason the Lord chose Abraham to make a covenant with was that He knew Abe would teach his children. We'll also touch upon coparenting.

Church and Ministry. I'll expand on our previous discussion of ministry as well as provide some guidelines for flourishing as a member of a local fellowship.

Job and Career. We'll look at applying the full range of spiritual insights to finding, keeping, and growing in your vocational pursuits. It may well be that all work and no play isn't good for us. I'll also address some perspectives on how to round out your life and bring another dimension of completeness into it.

Finances. I did say this one would be the last we'd talk about, but that doesn't mean it's not important. Minimizing the problems that money (or the lack thereof) can create is a huge issue in life.

Covenant and Sex

This can be a convoluted and difficult subject to approach when we ignore the essential principle of the Bible: the entire book is based on the concept of *covenant*. A covenant is an unbreakable agreement. Notice that I didn't put unbreakable in quotes or italics. In our culture, there is really no such thing as an unbreakable agreement, but in the culture of Bible lands, a covenant is a very real thing. It is an agreement made between two parties that, as long as the conditions are met, it can only be broken by the death of one of the covenant makers. If you have any experience as a believer, this will start to sound familiar to you. You may have even seen the Old and New *Testaments* referred to as the Old and New *Covenants*. Our salvation is based on this same principle of a covenant. It is foreshadowed in the Old Testament when Abraham "believed God," and his simple belief allowed God's righteousness to be credited to his life. (Take a look at Genesis 15–17 if you want to see how it all played out.) Jesus shed his blood to seal a promise that the Lord made, that by us believing, we could receive the gift of salvation. The remarkable thing about this covenant is that the Lord made it with himself! Think of what that means. Given the fact that God surely can't die, our covenant cannot be broken. Let that sink in before reading any further.

So how does this frame love and marriage? Let's start with sex. There is *so much* to say about the spiritual dimension to sex that it would be easier to write a separate book about it. But the major theme discussed in scripture verses, embedded in Bible stories, and woven into the culture of the people discussed in the Bible, is this: sex is a holy and sacred act. I'm tempted to say it again because it's quite likely something you've never heard before and perhaps do not even accept. God ordained this intimate physical experience as the mechanism by which a man and woman become "one flesh" and ratify their marriage covenant. It seals them together at a deep spiritual level way, way beyond their natural comprehension. At a neurobiological level, it connects neurons and releases neurotransmitters that develop a deep and abiding bond that neither person will probably recognize at a cortical level. This bonding process is why sex is reserved for marriage. Yep, I get it. How much more of an old-fashioned fuddy-duddy could I be than to suggest, in this day and age, that sex outside of marriage should be avoided? I really do get it. It's almost unconscionable even to talk about abstaining and such. But that doesn't mean it's incorrect. Now don't worry; I'm not going to start preaching to you about how wrong it is. In fact, "wrong" is not the issue. If, as believers in Jesus, we're going to convince people to live in a way that blesses their lives and helps them to avoid unnecessary heartache, we've got to do better than just telling them that things are wrong. Hopefully, our earlier discussion about sin and salvation makes it clear that we can be forgiven for the foolish things we do and that the Lord is not out to get us. Instead, God is living within us in the midst of our foolishness and stupidity, with the aim of leading us by his love. If you've ever read Psalm 23, this should make sense to you.

The point here is that having sex with someone you are not married to leaves a scar—both a spiritual and a neurobiological one. You see, as the bond takes place and then is not completed by staying connected to the person, the pulling away leaves a scar. In fact, people who have had multiple sex partners over time often find it difficult to later bond with the one they do want to marry because there is not enough "adhesive" left to make them "one flesh." The ripping and tearing from too many uncompleted bonds takes its toll. Appreciate once again that the message about sex being reserved for marriage is not as much an issue of "right versus wrong" as it is about understanding what the design of sex is in the context of a covenant. In the marriage covenant, outside the death of the husband or wife, the only other way that it can be broken is by adultery! Once another person enters their bond, the covenant no longer exists. If you look up the word *adulterate*, it will tell you that it means to "render something poorer in quality by adding an inferior substance to it." Am I starting to sound at least a *little* less like a fuddy-duddy? Sex and the marriage covenant are one and the same. You just shouldn't do one without the other!

Love and Marriage

So now with covenant under our belt, let's talk a little bit about marriage itself. Here again, writing a whole book on this is easier, so let me provide some guidelines so that I can cover the critical dimensions of this. But first, let me share a heartwarming experience.

Case Study: Khalil and Kiera

This will bless you if you believe that spirituality and romance can coexist. So Khalil was twenty-five at the time, and Kiera was twenty-four. Khalil's family did not attend church, but while he was in college, he accepted Jesus. We had known Kiera from grade school when her mom and dad became a part of the congregation. Khalil and Kiera were both involved in the life of the congregation—she worked with the children's ministry, and he sang and played the trumpet for the Praise Team—but never crossed paths outside of saying hello. One Sunday after service, Khalil asked if I had a minute before leaving. When we sat down to chat, he looked uncomfortable, almost embarrassed.

He said, "Pastor, what do you do when you like someone? I mean really, really like someone? I mean like you think you're falling in love with them?" I knew better than to ask the obvious question ("Who?"), so I told him first, of course, to pray for guidance and wisdom. I also said, "Keep your distance. Be careful about feeding an infatuation. Stay away and see how your feelings develop." He seemed content with this, and we agreed to stay in touch about it. About two weeks later, we got an email from Kiera. She relayed that she was wondering if we had some time to meet with her. She had an issue that she had talked to her parents about, and they suggested she get our input. We met for lunch near her job. She said (and you may already see this coming), "I think the Lord showed me my husband-to-be. What should I do?" After helping her assess exactly what she thought the Lord had shown her and how she could verify it, I'm sure you can guess what we said. Yep, the same thing we told Khalil because we believe it's the safest and best way to handle this situation.

The next time I talked with Khalil, of course, he revealed that it was Kiera! And Kiera's mom told Pastor Rita that it was Khalil. And I'm sure you can guess what ensued. Yep, they both kept their distance for about

> five months, and "it" wouldn't go away. Ultimately Khalil worked up the nerve to let Kiera know how he felt. And then six months later, they came for premarital counseling. They are still together today after twenty-two years. They did quiz Rita and me about how we could keep such a secret from them both for all that time! But you know as well as I do that it was vital that we not interfere and let it take its own course.
>
> So Khalil and Kiera are a bit fairy-tale-ish I agree. Other than this type of divine connection, how can sound biblical principles direct your path toward a fulfilling marriage? Here are the key principles:

Do not consider for marriage someone whose "faults" you believe you can correct over time. This is the most common mistake that you can make, and 90 percent of the time, it leads to frustration. The other 10 percent of the time, you end up with someone with too little self-respect for you to respect them. Frankly, everyone has the right to be who they are, and you have no right to try to change people to suit your needs. *Plus it won't work.* People are who they are, and although we all learn to modify our behavior, becoming someone else is a different matter. If you cannot see yourself embracing the person's total personality as it is right now, then he or she is probably not a good fit.

Don't let romance delude you totally. Absolutely you should have desire and passion, and fireworks should go off when you hear this person's name. After over forty years, I can still say that about Rita. But over time, things will simmer down, and though still intimate, your relationship will morph and broaden. The difficulties of life and the mistakes you will both make will require something much more powerful than romance: friendship. Friendship is what lasts. That deep respect and admiration for the other person will bear up under everything life can throw at you. Make sure that your relationship begins with, or at least develops, a profound basis of friendship before you consider making a covenant.

Don't base your choices on whom you can have a "good time" with. You are likely able to have a good time with any number of different types of people. Face it—it's not hard to have a good time. Though rewarding and fulfilling, much of life is not a "good time." It's a mix that includes sacrifice, hardship, loss, and challenges. You almost want to ask yourself whether you could have a "bad time" with that person. If you feel you could, that's a step toward reality. Note—even the best of friends may not have what it takes to handle conflict and trials. So yes, the requirement is a friendship that is tough enough to be tested.

Don't be drawn to someone who "worships the ground you walk on." Again, respect and admiration are essential, and for a while, it's fun to have that kind of starry-eyed celebrity status. At some point, the real you will emerge, and the pedestal will begin to shake! More so, as mentioned a moment ago, you will grow weary of someone who does not stand up for himself or herself and has no strong opinions. Marriage is about you being completed. The design in Genesis was that the male Adam be provided with an *ezer-kenegdo* ("help meet"). Although traditionally translated as a "helper," it is actually a "help." A "help" is fashioned to be stronger in your areas of weakness. So when we marry, we are joining together with someone who completes us by possessing strength where we may lack it. That is the design, and there are some subtle implications of being "completed."

Bible Study Challenge:

Read Psalms 121 to check out the characteristics of a "help". It's only 8 verses on so and will give you a sense of the strength that a covenant partner provides. The fact that he or she will likely be very different from you is an asset.

Someone who always agrees with you all the time guarantees that you will make bad decisions. So the design, again, generally causes you to be joined to someone who may be very different from you in lots of ways, especially thinking differently than you do. Certainly, you wouldn't want to marry someone who does not share your values and overall outlook on life. While a diversity of thought on the details is useful, it is not the same when it comes to the big picture. Our fundamental worldviews and our perspective on life are what drive our decisions. Discordance in this area will create conflict at a very high level, to the point that you will discover how different you are in a way that will be unsettling. If you share, even broadly, a fundamental worldview and perspective on life, the differences over details will become synergistic more often than they will be divisive.

Don't keep your feelings to yourself. He or she (especially she!) will know what's up even if you don't say anything. Recall our brief discussion about the deep neurobiological synapses that are a part of the bonding process. I'm going to use the idea of archetypes to talk about men and women. Clearly, you can't fairly generalize about gender. People don't fit nicely into a construct. If you were, however, to study the archetypal male brain versus the archetypal female brain, you'd see some glaring distinctions. The use of language is one that has a huge impact on marriage. The archetypal female brain has significantly increased activity between brain hemispheres. This results, for the most part, in the use of words to build intimacy and to process emotions. The archetypal male brain uses physical proximity in building intimacy and processes emotions internally. To the extent that a couple fits the archetype, their propensity for conversational details and the sharing of feelings may differ.

Without enough understanding of where you both are in this regard, you conceivably could have trouble communicating. "Little things" will become "big things," and the trust you have developed will get incrementally eaten away. Perhaps the most essential area where an inadequate level of communication skills will kill a relationship is not being able to know, express, or heal hurt feelings. This includes when you believe you have been wronged by the other person. You need to be able to get hurts out into the open. It's far better to have conflict in the "light of day" rather than inner hostilities in the "dark of night." You both must be able to forgive and to ask for forgiveness. Grudges eat away at the person who did the hurting and the one holding it.

Don't be selfish. This goes without saying, of course, but it can be easy to be selfish and not know it. Being *selfless* is a lifelong process, but it is critical to know what you are trying to accomplish through it. And so here comes what I believe to be a major truth of marriage and another huge key to happiness and fulfillment. Marriage is *not* about the other person making you happy. It's about you looking (i.e., asking the Lord) for ways to help and support *the other person* in fulfilling his or her purpose for being on the planet. In a good marriage, when both people are enabling each other to accomplish their purpose, everyone succeeds. In the process, they end up producing an atmosphere of extensive periods of peace, joy, and laughter. These periods are, again, only briefly punctuated with the normal difficulties that befall us. And because of the synergy produced through honoring the covenant, even the difficulties make a positive contribution.

A Word about Singleness

The prevailing attitude of our culture has been that marriage is the goal of family life. And within the church, it is assumed to be the pinnacle of spiritual sanctity. This is not only inaccurate but unfair to those of you who, for whatever reason, have remained single. The truth is that singleness is highly valued in the New Testament. (Bet you haven't heard that in a Sunday sermon. If you have, that's fabulous.) Don't misconstrue what I'm saying though—the Bible is clear that it's a good thing to get married too. The issue is always, What is the Lord's plan for your life? Being single, according to Paul, who remained unmarried himself, allows for an unhindered focus on the Lord's purposes. Your life can be just as full and enriching to others. So don't let the culture dictate how you feel about your status.

Parenting: Bending Trees

If you are led to have children, let's talk about the practical application of spiritual insights into raising children. Parenting is the most important job on the planet. You may be familiar with Proverbs 22:6, which says, "Train up a child in the way he should go: and when he is old, he will not depart from it." The word for *way* is *derek*. One of the meanings of *derek* is to bend something in a specific direction. A tree will grow in a particular direction based on the ground it's planted in, and what it must do to get access to enough sunlight and water. It will *bend itself* in that direction. So think of this proverb telling us that children are already "bent" in a certain direction according to the Lord's purpose for their lives. Somewhat like the concept of marriage, a parent's job is to identify the "bent" of their children and facilitate the development of their purpose. If you put them anywhere near the path they are supposed to be on, the proverb says that they will then grow into the completeness of it.

Case Study: Donald and Belinda

If there were ever two people that functioned on the genius level, it would be this husband and wife. Donald has a PhD in nuclear physics and is working at a US Army development laboratory. Belinda is a professor of computational biology at a prestigious university in the Washington, DC, area. (She wrote her dissertation on Chinese number theory—whatever that actually is!) In addition to being intellectuals and scientists, they have a deep love of God and see their faith perfectly expressed in their professions. They also have two talented children—Rosemarie, sixteen, and Salvatore, fourteen—who are very good students. At the moment, though, they are both troubled kids.

Here's what I think has happened. Rosemarie is tall like her dad, and after being "recruited" to play basketball in middle school, she excelled at the sport. She is beginning to get offers from colleges for both basketball and volleyball. Salvatore, on the other hand, can pick up pretty much any musical instrument and *teach himself* how to play. He's a serious guitarist and pianist and can hold his own on the drums. You'd think this kind of talent would be a blessing, but not to Don and Belinda. They are scientists. While the kids do well in school, the idea of pursuing an athletic scholarship (as Rosemarie wants to do) or applying to a conservatory (as Salvatore has begun to discuss) is untenable to them. They had already decided when the kids were born that they would pursue college and careers in one of the STEM fields (science, technology, engineering, and math). To them, right now, there is no other option for their son or daughter.

At one of our last discussions, Don, out of his frustration, threw up his hands and told Rosemarie she was "throwing her life away with sports" and that "ladies" who were athletes were not really ladies. When Sal came to his sister's defense, both Don and Belinda began to preach to him about how all musicians were drug addicts, and they didn't want him to end up that way. Rosemarie called her dad a "pompous ass" who was out of touch with reality. Sal said to them both, "Bite me if you don't like what I want to do. I'd rather be a junkie musician than live in this house another day!" Ugly all the way around.

We're still in the throes of this situation, so I don't have a nice, neat conclusion to offer you. I can tell you this. The level of rebellion and borderline disrespect Rosemarie and Salvatore show their mom and dad is clearly not good. Worse yet, Mom and Dad have lost their cool more than a few times in trying to reason with them.

It's hard not to empathize with all parties in this family drama, but at the end of the day, Mom and Dad are going to have to find a way to negotiate a settlement. If they keep devaluing their children's gifts and talents, they will break them. If they do not appreciate what seems to be some degree of "bent" in their children, they will crush their dreams.

It's also not fair to say that Don and Belinda should have discerned the direction their kids needed to go. As children are growing up, they will hopefully express an interest and try all kinds of things before they settle on something firm. The key, though, is to know from the outset that deciding for them based on your own preferences alone may not be as useful. It can take time to uncover a child's bent. The key is to provide them with the skill sets to have options when they reach a place where life decisions need to be made. Too many parents do not learn what parenting is about and put unnecessary limitations and boundaries on their children's future.

Parenting, in any dimension, is an awfully hard job. While it perhaps can never be done perfectly, there are some clear guidelines you can follow. Here is a pretty comprehensive list of them:

Learn what is expected of children at different age categories. Unrealistic expectations of what children should be doing at different stages make it hard for parents and even harder for children. You have to know your child, of course, but appreciating approximate child-development stages is eye-opening. I'd love to cover each one now, but as a parent, you need to do some homework! And it's easy to find resources. Just google "stages of child development."

Establish the family's values. Remember my story of the influence my family has had on my sense of "chosen-ness"? Being a Thompson was always something that had meaning growing up. Even the contributions of my incredible granddaddy on my mom's side solidified that identity. Again, it didn't make me any better than the folks next door or across the street. Being a Thompson just anchored me and imparted resilience. And of course, I passed along to my children the special sense of being Thompsons. This is a great family activity. Imagine getting together with the kids and talking about what your family's values are. What makes us special? What are the distinctive features of this household that nourish us? What makes coming through our front door meaningful? You'll want to keep your list of values as short and as simple as possible. The list makes a great refrigerator poster if your children are into that sort of thing.

Establish some rules. Most parents have forgotten what children, deep down inside, associate rules with. On the surface, rules are restrictive, inconvenient, and are associated with punishment because there are usually consequences for breaking them. Deep down inside, children associate rules with love. They know and appreciate, on a subliminal level, the fact that people who don't care about them don't take the time to restrict their behavior. But we forget as we get older, I think. For example, think back to the teacher or coach who just would not get off your case. This person hounded you relentlessly to put forward your best effort and pressured you when you fell short. Your coach was an absolute pain. I had a lot of these teachers and coaches, praise the Lord. I can remember seeing one of them coming toward me and turning around in the hall and heading the other direction just to avoid the person! But now, how do you and I feel about those rabid rule-makers? Yep, whether we liked it at the time or not, we now know how much they cared about us.

You don't need too many rules. The rule-making process should also be a family activity, just like developing your values. It's also a great idea to use the same setting to agree on the consequences that attend the rules. Now here's where a biblical approach sets itself apart from the worldly norm. Not only are we going to agree on the negative consequences—what happens when you don't keep the rules—but we're also going to agree on the positive consequences. The idea of being rewarded for doing the right thing is probably a more powerful motivator than punishment for doing the wrong thing. Instilling the idea that obedience can bring a blessing is a foundational truth in scripture as well. Let your children know that you are more interested in catching them doing something right than you are in punishing them for doing something wrong. Keep in mind that these positive consequences should not be huge, and they should be sustainable. And remember, they are children. It will take a little time for the lessons to have an impact. But they will.

Case Study: Joey

I've done a fair amount of jail ministry. In jail ministry, you're working with someone who will eventually be released and will have another chance to make better decisions. "Joey" was a young man in his late twenties who had been in and out of detention since he was fourteen. He was very, very bright but had just this tinge of angry indignation. Up until he was thirteen, he was an honor roll student and was gifted at writing and languages. He spoke fluent Spanish, had a good grasp of German and Italian, and could hold his own in French! When he turned thirteen, he yielded to the pressure and decided to join the gang. He was "jacked in" by breaking in someone's home and stealing enough for it to qualify as grand larceny. Later that night, he ran the gauntlet and was accepted as a member. (The gauntlet is when you pass between a line of fellow gang members who are allowed to punch and kick you. You have to make it to the end of the line on your feet.)

Somehow I developed a rapport with him. Joey said I was "straight up," and he felt comfortable telling me the truth about what he was thinking and feeling. He was down to eight months on his sentence and had planned to leave once he got out. He was born and raised in the area but agreed to listen to his older sister's advice and move out to the Midwest to live with her and get reestablished. He has six siblings, and he is the next to the oldest. Joey had reached the point where gang life had run its course, and the only way to not end up back in jail or worse was to get as far away as he could.

I was always amazed at the idea that kids as smart as Joey could end up in a gang. And whenever I feel they want to talk about it, I ask them. Joey's response was akin to the rest. He said he needed a "family."

"But, Joey, you told me your mom and dad tried their best to provide for you and took care of you well," I said in one of our conversations. And they had. His dad worked a steady construction job. He did have an alcohol problem but was never abusive toward him, his siblings, or his mom. She worked two jobs—as a dental assistant from 7:00 a.m. to 3:00 p.m. and then as the registrar at the community college from 4:00 p.m. to 10:00 p.m. on the weekends. So what went wrong?

Joey accepted full responsibility for his decisions and did not blame his parents. He did say, though, that, because they were so busy, a couple of things were missing. For one, he said, "It seems they hardly noticed

> anything I did that was good. I know that being expected to do well in school and everything is normal, but it would have been nice to have gotten a pat on the head or to have been openly congratulated when I got mostly A's on a report card. It would have made me feel better about myself, especially when I was ten or so. The biggest thing, though, is that there weren't any rules. I mean, you'd think with all these kids, there'd be some strictness somewhere, but there wasn't. If one of us got in trouble, you'd get yelled at or get a spanking, but it was never made clear in the beginning what to do or not do."
>
> Apparently, gang life is just the opposite. There are a *lot* of rules—not good ones, of course—but there are a lot. And it's that abundance of rules, according to Joey, and the other young men I've met with, that causes them to see the gang as a "family."
>
> "In a strange way," Joey quipped, "it really felt like people cared about you just because they had rules."

Figure Out Their "Currency"

Parents have to do a lot of disciplining to raise their children well. An important insight is the idea of "currency." Everyone has a shortlist of things that are important for a sense of fulfillment. *Currency* is a term to express this. For example, I have a grandson who just *loves* technology. If things go south, you can put him in time-out all day, and it won't be that big of a deal. But make the use of his iPad the bargaining chip for obedient behavior? To him, that's an entirely different thing. Technology is his *currency*. Knowing currency is both a way to reward as well as to enact negative consequences and is the most sustainable way to get behavior change. Corporal punishment is a profound penalty (and it hurts) but has proven not to be a good source of behavior change, not to mention the potential for overdoing it when under pressure or stressed.

Praise Your Children

As early as six months, look for legitimate and authentic opportunities to congratulate them on any good thing they do, especially if it aligns with a behavior you want them to repeat. At other times, especially before bedtime, tell them how glad you are to be their mom or dad (other types of guardians follow suit). These unconditional positives will enhance their self-esteem and build their resilience as they get older and face life's challenges. Obviously, you need to be judicious in the frequency and timing. Make it legitimate and authentic. But do it.

Teach Them to Teach Themselves

The downfall of your current public education system has been that it was originally developed to prepare people to take their place within a defined system. In an industrial age, it was important to possess a solid set of basic skills and learn the value of conforming to organizational norms. Clearly, that aspect of the culture has changed. Even if your education is intended to prepare you to hold a job, you need to be a "knowledge worker" regardless. In addition, the transformation of our culture has also made it necessary for the public system to take on an entire spectrum of education that used to be done at home. My purpose is not to say whether that's a good thing or not but only to make the point that the system is overwhelmed. So that means that, as a parent, you must step in and play perhaps a different role in your children's education: teach them how to teach themselves!

The first step is to cultivate a love for learning that is already present in most children. Don't depend on the school to do this. Again, not only do they have their hands full, but their primary role is teaching your children certain *things*, not creating elasticity in their brains. And because kids come with this innate desire to explore, there's a very straightforward strategy here:

Get them reading. Begin by reading to them and then making sure they learn to read as early as possible. Treat books (digital or otherwise) as great adventures. It's even better when they see you reading. They'll begin to imitate your behavior.

Travel. Seeing another part of the world, being amid people who are different from what you're used to, eating their food, etc. all serve powerfully to expand children's idea of how big the world is. It also expands their sense of what is possible. If you don't have the means to take them to a foreign country, get on the bus, and take them to a foreign neighborhood.

Akin to traveling is to expose them to as many unique experiences as you can. Again money is not the issue. Most museums are free. Cultural and community organizations hold a plethora of enrichment activities.

Capture teachable moments. Look for every opportunity you can to use everyday situations and circumstances to impart some curiosity. Whet their appetite to know more, and encourage them to find out on their own. Make learning fun, and like any kid, they will want to do more of it.

And Then There's Coparenting

So sometimes it doesn't work out. It's hard enough for the man and the woman, and it can be tragic when children are involved. Contrary to popular opinion, God's disdain for the breaking of a covenant is only surpassed by the offer of healing and restoration for all the parties involved. (There are a number of nuances of what should happen once you get divorced in terms of remarriage and the like. I'll save that for another book!) But it is the children whose needs should be first attended to. As an outgrowth of my ministry efforts, I teach a class mandated by our state Supreme Court. Parents getting divorced or separated are required to take it. They learn about the potentially traumatic effects of a divorce/separation on children at various age categories and what to do to prevent it. I don't have time and space to cover all aspects of it, but I will distill just a few of the essentials. I'd obviously encourage you to take such a class if you find yourself in a coparenting role.

Because of God's grace, once again, life can still be whole and complete. So here goes:

Understand how anger works. People are essentially rendered incapable of rational thought and action if their anger exceeds a certain level. If you are angry about what your coparent did to you, it will take some time before you can easily handle things. Avoid big decisions, and find productive ways to get rid of it. Anger is toxic. If your coparent is angry, try not to expect too many things to go well until the anger subsides below that level.

Shift your focus. Many times, the agony of a failed relationship keeps us focused on it. Worse yet, an angry and frustrated coparent will try to force us into emotional tugs of war. If you want to help your children the most, stop expending your emotional energy on that relationship and instead focus exclusively on your children. This can make a huge difference. When you're focused on the relationship, there are some things you will absolutely say and do to deal with the impacts. If you are "child-focused," you will think twice about what you say or do.

Stop arguing in front of your child. This is the *biggest* thing that tears kids apart. In most cases, they are equal parts of both of you, and hearing you two exchange harsh words is like them being criticized. Over time, when the anger dips lower, coparents can learn to negotiate in ways that avoid ugly words and still allow for the truth to be told.

Don't keep your coparent from his or her children. It should go without saying that this assumes the other person is fit to be a parent. And it also goes without saying that if you are angry and relationship-focused, this will look like the best way to get back at him or her. Obviously, the problem is that it is your child that is being hurt. There are reams of research documents that will validate the seemingly simple truth that Mom and Dad are different and that a child needs an equal portion of both.

Case Study: Fallon Lucas

Fallon just turned thirty-four. He's been a member of the congregation for eight years now. You'd never guess that he's never taken a vocal class before when you hear him sing. He loves the Lord and is dedicated to serving in any way he can. His service at church is a good cover for the deep-seated anger that continues to eat away at him. You see, his parents got divorced when he was eight, and he's never gotten over it. It's a story I'm sure you've heard too many times. I'll spare you the details, but in this version, it was his father who was the primary author of the trauma, although it always takes two. Not only did he leave for another woman, but he also married her just eighteen months later. The traumatic part was that to appease his new wife, he had very little contact with Fallon and never gave him any reason for the distance.

In one of our conversations about all this, Fallon said, "I could easily come to grips with why he left my mom, but why me too?" Despite his insensitivity, his father wasn't a monster. He just was ignorant of the impact that the divorce would have if he didn't attend to his son's need for help in creating a "new normal." Fallon's anger showed up in lots of ways and continues to do so. For example, he barely made it out of high school and, although a smart kid, would not even entertain the idea of college. He attempted several vocational trades from cybersecurity to being a security guard. He excelled in all of them until he had to take instructions from a boss. Fallon is aware that he has inadvertently convinced himself that messing up his own future is the best way to get back at his father. Even mild trauma has a way of horribly twisting our thinking. His struggle now is to undo that thought process. The saddest part of this is that it wouldn't have taken much at all for his father to have prevented this. He just didn't know.

There is, of course, a much longer list of strategies, tools, and competencies to create a viable coparenting environment. My experience is that if you can't manage these basics, it's really tough and takes a much longer time. These few things also get us to a place where we can embrace the Holy Spirit's role in our own restoration. All that is asked is summed up in Paul's words to the Romans, verse 18 of chapter 12: "If possible, so far as it depends on you, be at peace with all men" (NASB version). Sometimes it seems barely possible, but *time* is the best friend of failed relationships. You'll be surprised what the two of you are capable of once the anger goes away.

"Church" Life

It is obvious that I am postulating that there is an order to things. Our culture, once again, seems to have developed an aversion for appreciating the design within which life is lived to its fullest. Order, from a biblical and spiritual viewpoint, is even less well understood. The prevailing mentality is that biblical order is intended to stifle our expression. Nothing could be further from the truth, of course. Order provides freedom and protection.

There are a lot of religious groups that believe that the order in your life begins with your church involvement. The Bible has a totally different slant on this. For one, the writers of the New Testament did not *go to* church. They understood themselves *to be* the church. So separating your spiritual life from the rest of life is an unbiblical concept. Secondly, the scriptures indicate that your family unit, however it is constructed, is the focal point for your ministry, not just the congregation you attend. A radical thought perhaps, but if so, then Paul is radical. He told Timothy in 1 Timothy 5 that you disqualify yourself from ministry if you do not first take care of your family and your relatives. I also mentioned

Abraham earlier. More specifically, in Genesis 18, we are informed that one of the reasons that the Lord chose Abram to a father of many nations is that he would be automatically compelled to bring up his children in the same manner as he had been led by the Lord. Order your life properly then, and make sure your family is your first ministry and your chief priority. This works out perfectly anyway because the spiritual development and health of your family is the key to "echad."

Joining a Congregation

I'd like you to notice that the heading does not say "finding a church." Recall our previous discussion of the church having erroneously become a "place" rather than a "people." When the sixty or so King James translators were commissioned in 1604, they were given a list of guidelines. Most of those guidelines were to govern the translation logistics and to facilitate the editing process. One such guideline dictated that the original names of the Old Testament prophets remain in their original pronunciation. A final one mandated that any time the word *ecclesia* appeared, it was to be rendered as "church." Subtle, right? Well you see, *ecclesia* refers to a group of people who have been "called out" as if to assemble themselves for a specific purpose. The correct translation would be "congregation." The word *church* isn't even Greek but Latin. It refers to a physical temple where idol worship took place. And so our idea of what we're supposed to be doing as believers has been distorted for at least four hundred years.

At the same time, we are supposed to assemble ourselves together on a regular basis. Outside of me whining about translation errors, my point is that you should be looking to join a community of believers, a congregation. Regardless of the denomination, size, or doctrinal slant, I'm suggesting you join with a group of believers where there is a genuine sense of community. I'm going to do the hardest thing possible now, and that is to provide some objective criteria for you to consider. Two things first: (1) I think I've made my biblical biases clear enough that you can filter these suggestions; and (2) the Lord has a place for you in the Body of Christ, so above all, pray and follow the leading of the Lord.

You should be able to feel the love soon after you walk through the door. If you don't, then your "Spidey-senses" should begin to tingle. People should be actively willing to greet you and not let you walk out the door without engaging you even mildly. Give it three visits or so though before forming an absolute opinion. Congregations have off days too.

Look for a good balance between "preaching" (exhortation and encouragement) and "teaching" (instruction on the basics of the Bible and how to live your faith). Good preaching is awesome, but at some point, you need some substance to grow in the Lord. Also, as a pastor, "teaching" you what I think I understand the Bible to say can be different from "telling" you what you should believe.

You'll want to stay in tune with how well the basic messages that are being transmitted line up with the core of what the Bible says. Let me emphasize the "core." You're not likely to find a place where everything is accurate. I mean, first of all, there are so many things that we don't even understand, to begin with. Secondly, we really don't have to agree on everything either. It's okay to have variations on the theme on peripheral issues. But the core has to be close to the mark. Salvation must be by grace through faith, forgiveness must be available to all, God must be loving in the same way that Jesus was, the cross must be sufficient, and so on. If these core elements deviate too far, you're simply talking about another faith; that's all.

Keep your eyes on how "pastor centered" it is. We do have a leadership role, and it should be clear who we are. But if you can't ask him or her to explain something, professionally disagree with his or her point of view, or raise a question over something that was said . . .

Look for an emphasis on identifying, supporting, and developing the various gifts and talents in the congregation. Revisit the study challenge on Ephesians Chapter 4, especially verses 11–14, back in chapter 2. There are of course varying degrees of emphasis on this idea of developing people, but if it's not present at all, then that would be concerning. If all they want from you is for you to be a spectator, that's not healthy. Never mind the biblical error.

Being a "Minister"

Assuming your congregation puts the emphasis on this, living your faith is what it's all about. Sundays are great times, but the heart of the matter is what happens the rest of the days of the week, right? And we've already talked about how traditional church history has mistakenly minimized the role of individual members through an inordinate affection with titles. What this means is that we must recognize that *wherever the Lord places you will likely be a place of ministry.* I feel like even if half of the body of Christ got this, we could literally change the world. As strange as this may sound, the heart of the gospel is that Jesus, through the agency of the Holy Spirit, is living his life through you. Everywhere you go, every person you come in contact with is designed to create an opportunity for the kingdom of God to be expanded. Sometimes we are called upon to do something or say something. Many, many times we are called upon just to be "present" with the sensitivity and inherent understanding that we are there on purpose. Look. I can appreciate that once again this sounds a bit over the top. But it is so vital that you grasp how important you are in the Lord's plan. And although we are not robots or marionette puppets being manipulated every waking moment, every waking moment is pregnant with the Lord's desire that everyone comes into the knowledge of His unfathomable love for them. And as crazy as it seems, there is no plan B. You and I are it.

> ### Case Study: Marjorie the Magnet
>
> Honestly, even as a pastor, I got tired of hearing her complain about her job! Marjorie is a valued member of the congregation and always has a word of

encouragement for folks. She's survived breast cancer and her husband's near-fatal automobile accident and held her younger sister's hand through a three-year struggle to overcome prescription drug addiction. She's definitely not one of those chronic complainers, but her place of employment had been a "cross to bear," as she put it, from the moment she was hired (seventeen years ago) until she got a revelation (two and a half years ago). Granted, it's a tough place. She works as a senior supervisor in the customer service division of a large industrial appliance company. Her manager apparently has no managerial skill, and Marjorie has fourteen customer-service reps reporting to her. I'm sure some of you can relate to this as it is far too common. The stress is unbearable at times, with often over fifty active complaint cases being handled. Almost half of those are face-to-face encounters. Not only do her fourteen folks come to her regularly to find solace, but because of the poor management, Marjorie estimated that something like thirty different employees come to her to complain and share their problems, work-related and personal.

Up until two years ago, she had been "begging" God for another job. But every opportunity she pursued came to naught. Her frustration had reached such a peak that early one morning, a coworker was already sitting in her office when she arrived. The poor guy just started in about all his issues. In exasperation, Marjorie stopped him midsentence and blurted, "Why do *all* of you bother me *all* the time with *all* your problems!" In the intervening silence, she realized she was close to losing it, and as she started to apologize, he responded, "Geez, Marj, you just seem to handle all the crap around here so well. You're always smiling, you never lose your cool, and you always seem to have such good insights no matter what the trouble is. I don't know. You have this air about you like you're always at peace. Folks are just drawn to the way you seem to deal with life. I know I wish I had some of that peace." Then came the revelation. This *was* her ministry. The Lord had sent her into a "dark place" so that she could be the light. The resilience that she had developed had been used by the Holy Spirit to advance the kingdom! For the two and a half years since her epiphany, she goes to work *expecting* people to come to her. And although she is respectful of the unspoken prohibition to not evangelize on the job, she has found a way for people to connect with her outside work. She has led six people to accept Jesus as their Lord and Savior. She is currently waiting for management's approval for a lunchtime Bible study that her coworkers have requested without her even knowing about it. Of course, they want her to lead it.

While the colloquial expression "Bloom where you are planted" is not found in the Bible, it is still great advice for fulfilling the Lord's purposes.

Job and Career

Marjorie's story is the perfect segue. The role of work in our lives, in general, is an extremely important topic. Most of us spend so much time there, even when we may not enjoy what we do. In fact, an awful lot of the pressures we face are related to work. This makes this prime territory for you and me to see the power of God show up and for the wisdom of the scriptures to guide us toward success. Life, and especially career, is *all about options*. This is where the biblical admonitions concerning planning mesh with the idea of seeking the Lord's purposes.

Study Challenge:

Dig into Luke 14 (especially verses 28–33) and Proverbs 3, 16 and 21. You'll see that the idea of planning and

> preparing is just as spiritual as praying and seeking. At the end of the day, of course, we believe that the Holy Spirit will take our meager and sometimes misguided efforts and direct us along the right way. But you have to be in motion to be directed.

Four Major Issues to Address in Career Planning

If you're just starting out or sensing the Lord is beckoning you to make a change, there's some high-level thinking that is useful in sharpening your focus. The first is, *What have you prepared yourself to do?* I can't tell you how many people Rita and I have counseled who are disgruntled because the job or career direction they desire is out of reach at the moment. For example, they want a position that requires a college degree, and for whatever reason, they don't have one. Hindsight being 20/20, I would be wasting your time harping on what you should have done. Yet there's no way around the fact that you need to develop some strategic-thinking skills and prepare yourself.

Now what's worse than the people I just mentioned are the ones who aren't even willing to begin where they are and work toward what's required. This is where our discussion of being able to teach oneself pays huge dividends. Look. Life is not only too short, but it makes absolutely *no sense* to settle for less than the Lord's best. A lot of times, the desire you have came from the Lord because you have already immersed yourself in His grace. (See Psalm 37:4–6 so that I may avoid further pontification.)

Second thing, *What are your demonstrated competencies?* In other words, what have you proven that you are truly good at? Having a foundation to spring from can be crucial in getting a foot in the door. You'll want to be able to express the results you produced in these areas. Once you get to the résumé or job-interview stages, being able to "quantify" your competencies will cause you to stand out. Most people just don't do this. When you take stock of what you have prepared yourself to do, don't overlook gifts and talents that may have been used in a job or career capacity. Part of making a change quite often is when the Lord brings forth something in you that has been dormant or underutilized in the past. Keep in mind, therefore, that the Holy Spirit is always way out ahead of us.

Third, *What is it that you enjoy doing?* Silly question on the surface but you must concede that there are way too many folks who dislike their jobs. I'm using *dislike* just to avoid being blunter. And you know I'm right. There is a staggering number of believers who go to work and come home day after day, week after week, and year after year, never feeling like they have done anything that counts. I have to tell you, hopefully without sounding like I'm congratulating myself, that at the tender age of seventeen, I refused to go down that path. I patently refused to end up doing something that I didn't like or didn't provide a sense of value. I had great training on this. My mom and dad taught me to work hard, to build, and to not put limits on myself. So I'm not saying that everything should always be *fun*. But to me, *enjoying* doesn't always insist on the fun. Rant over.

Honestly though, take careful stock of what enjoyment looks like. Here are some examples of the categories of interest you might want to consider:

Are looking for a way to produce income or a "career"?

If you are looking to produce income, do you want to do it as part of an organization or as your business?

If you're looking to produce income as part of an organization, do you have the skills or expertise that have value or that can be monetized?

If you're looking to produce income as your own business, do you have the mentality and fortitude?

If you're looking for a career, do you prefer to work with things or with people?

If it's people, do you want to be in a support role or on the front lines?

If it's things, what skills or expertise do you have that can add value?

What type of work environment fits you? Are you a nine-to-five person, or do you prefer a more varied schedule?

Do you need to be among others, or do you prefer to work remotely or virtually?

You may surprise yourself at the options that open up, especially again if your job/career analysis is taking place as a result of the need or opportunity to make a change.

Case Study: Out of the Ashes

Some divorce situations are uglier than others. This was certainly the case with "Mr. Mike." We all call him "mister" because he has this regal, polished, and incredibly gracious air about him. Mr. Mike joined the congregation after being invited by a friend to get prayer for a deadly bacterial infection he had picked up on a business trip to Guyana. He was ultimately healed of the infection and went on to become a dedicated member of the congregation. Remember Lydia? He's the male version! He has that same gift of hospitality. He is an amazing chef, entertainer, event planner—you name it. His zeal for serving the Lord was well received by his wife. The two of them had traveled the world together in his capacity as a foreign service officer. She was a churchgoer and a nominal member of a congregation but did not get to the idea of living a life of faith. But she was supportive of his involvement and attended occasionally.

One weekday Mr. Mike got in early from a trip to New York, only to find her in bed with a colleague of his. As the story unraveled, they had been carrying on a six-year affair and made plans to divorce their spouses and remarry. Of course, Mr. Mike was devastated. Even with the help and support of the congregation, he sank into a deep depression culminating with him resigning from his foreign service post. Over a year later, he finally regained his balance and went about the task of rebuilding his life. What occurred to him more than anything was the lack of desire to get back into the fast-paced, stress-filled world of international diplomacy. He mentioned to me that he had lost his "edge." In some respects, he blamed the extensive travel on not attending enough to his ex-wife's needs.

"The divorce just took away such a big piece of me," he would lament, "but what else do I know?"

By now, you have probably caught onto the rhythm of these stories I have been sharing. The plot goes one way or the other. Either they fail to comprehend the Lord's love for them and they wallow in the muck, or they get a revelation and rise from the ashes toward greater heights. Mr. Mike rose. And you can also, by now, figure out where he found his new beginning. Yep, he started his own event-management and catering business! A church member even came alongside to create a social media campaign where he shares easy recipes for people to enjoy dishes from all over the world. Not only he is doing great business-wise, but he has found a new sense of satisfaction and a greater fullness in his life than what he had experienced before the divorce. These stories are *not* uncommon for those who put their faith, and their future, in the Lord's hands, no matter what they have been through.

Achieving the Breadth of Satisfaction

Mr. Mike was also very fortunate in finding a career option that satisfied him in a complete way. But that is not always the case. I have come to believe that one of the major reasons that so many people have such disdain for their jobs is because it is not able to satisfy the full range of their needs as a person. While every place we are sent will provide an opportunity for our ministry to express itself, every place we are sent is not necessarily intended to satisfy the depth of our personality. For example, in a very healthy way, I think we all need a sense of importance, the feeling that what we are doing is contributing to something we value. Some jobs or even careers can have a limited impact on that aspect of our being. There is probably a long list of intangible things that make you feel worthwhile, valuable, or productive.

Because of this, you will want to look for ways to round out your life. Real success and satisfaction will be when the full range of your needs and interests have an outlet. This is where involvement in the life of the congregation for lots of people is huge. Suppose you are a front-line operator in a manufacturing plant with no supervisory or leadership role. And at the same time, you have a real urge and capacity to organize and motivate people. When you can find an outlet for that side of you by being in charge of the men's ministry, it becomes an especially satisfying experience.

I have personal experience with this. I am a *very* competitive person. I'm a good sport and gracious (though mildly disappointed loser—OK, more than mildly disappointed, but never obnoxious). I found a healthy and productive outlet for this side of my personality by coaching athletics. I already told you about coaching youth-club soccer. I also did high school lacrosse for eleven years and college lacrosse for twelve. Along the way, I had both indirect and direct opportunities for my ministry to express itself. I remember being asked when I was coaching at the college level why, with everything else I had going on, I would make such a commitment. My humorous response was that, as a pastor and a consultant, I never got to yell! Not sure they realized how honest I was being.

You certainly can overdo it and end up being so busy that your outlets drain life from you rather than produce life in you. This is where understanding your needs and taking stock in a deliberate way becomes helpful. I'm at the stage now where I'm consciously reducing the amount of stuff I'm doing. My needs and sources of satisfaction are changing. Reserving time for the spontaneity of my kids' and grandkids' schedule, hanging out with Rita, and preparing for the next career all are vitally important to me. The Bible talks a lot about seasons. When we can synch up with the ebb and flow of the Holy Spirit's movement through our lives, we become more sensitive to the need to make changes. I don't see myself doing less, just doing more of what produces the most satisfaction, the most shalom, the most echad.

Finances

I promised we'd save the discussion of money for the last. It is the lowest form of satisfaction and prosperity there is, but it is, of course, still important. Jesus talked a *lot* about money and the related issues of possessions and material gain. It is so very sad that ministries talk way too much about money. (I'm tempted to go into another rant—this time about TV preachers and the obvious scams that give legitimate ministers such a bad name. I won't.) Jesus talked about money because there are important spiritual truths involved. There is a huge benefit in handling your finances in a biblical fashion. Here are a few of the concepts that serve as the foundation of what we'll discuss here.

Money is *not* the root of all evil. The *love of money* is. This is saying that if "things" have your heart, then you won't be able to embrace the gospel fully.

If you develop an attitude of giving, you will always live in abundance. This is not just true of money. Jesus knew how important it was to people and that, if you could learn to be generous with money, it would open your heart to a lifestyle of giving. In other words, be a charitable person, and you will never have any money problems. (This is a spiritual "law" that has changed the lives of so many people I have encountered as a pastor.)

Make as much as you are entitled to without sacrificing what is important to you and important for those who love you. No, it doesn't do any good to gain the whole world and lose your soul.

If you spend all your time worrying about how to keep it and how to get more, it will slip through your fingers like sand.

Please, please, please don't let the excessive hype around money that you may have heard from certain parts of the body of Christ dissuade from believing that these principles work. I haven't talked about the influence of evil forces at all, but just let me say that this is one area where the truth-twisting and perverted motives are profound. Overlay that with a culture that is materialistic, to begin with, and it is easy to understand why folks shun the institutional church's preoccupation with money.

There's one other dimension to this too. In very subtle ways, the materialistic message can appeal to people as a way of absolving their misplaced guilt. Let me explain this quickly. We've already discussed God's grace and how your own efforts to gain the Lord's favor are useless. Jesus took care of that. Well, if you don't get this, then it's very easy to subconsciously give as a way of appeasing the wrath that you subconsciously believe is being attached to your failures and shortcomings. People can give for the wrong reasons, even when they are not being pressured.

Study Challenge:

Read 2 Corinthians 9. I'd also recommend you use a translation that is easy to understand to get the gist of what is being said here. Verse 7 is the key point I'm hoping gets across.

Given these issues and the biblical foundation, let's talk about some basic, sound money principles:

1. Budgeting
2. Giving
3. Saving
4. Protecting
5. Investing
6. Structuring

Have Some Sort of Budget

I should tell you that this is one of those areas I have struggled with over time, especially in my earlier years. Neither Rita nor I are big spenders, nor are we in love with stuff. (OK, I do have a weakness for kitchen gadgets and innovations in technology.) But when it came to keeping track of it, some sort of attention-deficit thing kicks in. However, the fact that I have struggled I think helps qualify me even more as someone whose advice you should take. Any form of budget will do. You simply want to know and stay on top of how your income from all sources and your expenses stay in line each month. You'll also want to factor in money for taxes that could accrue outside what may be deducted from a paycheck, money you will save, and money you will set aside for giving. The more detailed you can be about expenses, the better it can all be tracked. Find a balance between complexity and manageability. An important lesson I painfully learned was to have a budget process that you can easily manage. Even if you don't have the discipline to do it proactively, use a banking tool that will tell you how you spend money. It's the only way to monitor your priorities and make sure they are aligned. Back in the day, we didn't have the endless array of budgeting and financial management tools that I can now operate from my phone.

You will also want to support your budgeting and financial-management process with a good record-keeping and tax-payment system. If this isn't your forte, it is worth it to get some help here. Boy, I wish I had heeded this earlier on. It took me *way* too long to come to this realization. I am very well-versed in business. I understand accounting, and I had all the skills required to do this part well. But it just wasn't my strong suit. I struggled miserably and unnecessarily with record keeping and tax stuff until I finally admitted that I needed help to do this right.

Give Consistently

We've already covered this in part, so I just want to accent a couple of things and provide you with a few practical guidelines. Naturally, my own primary focus is giving to support the congregation and other ministry efforts. Within the body of Christ, there is the concept of tithes and offerings. *Tithe* means "a tenth." It is the custom of giving 10 percent of your income to the congregation. The Old Testament concept was naturally based on agriculture and farming since that's where people's "treasure" was produced. An "offering" is thus taken to mean any giving above the tithe.

Currently, there are a lot of controversies in some quarters about whether tithing is required or even valid in the New Testament. I have no problem addressing controversies, but honestly, the time it would take here wouldn't be worth it. Let me say this instead. There are a lot of us that have a New Testament revelation and understanding of tithing, and so we do it. I also have very good friends who don't believe in tithing at all. The remarkable thing is that some of them who don't believe in it end up giving much more than 10 percent! So at the end of the day, this is something you and the Lord need to get clear on between the two of you.

Wherever you end up, here are some ways of looking at the broad spectrum of giving:

Be uncomfortable when you are pressured, promised, or guilted into giving in any setting. For example, I would be wary of a minister who tells you that the Lord will do "XYZ" for you if you give. That's not the gospel. I would be equally wary of a charity that tells you how many children won't eat if you don't help.

Know where the money is going. This is easier for charities than for ministries or congregations. The key figure for charities is the administrative percentage. That equates to how much of your donation goes to overhead expenses and how much goes directly to help people. Lots of times, when you decide to give to support relief after a natural disaster, let's say, the administrative burden for large charities can be significant enough that you might be better off finding a more local organization to support. Ministries are more guarded. Here we talk about "good ground," a take-off on the parable of the sower. (You can find it in Matthew 13, Mark 4, or Luke 8.) Look for ministries that have a track record of effectiveness in the areas you are inclined to support. Within a congregation, it can get even touchier. Be relieved when they are open about the finances. After all, the money belongs to the congregation, not the pastor. Be patient if they are not necessarily forthcoming with the information or uncomfortable with questions. At some point, though, they should be willing to share. We share all the details on our congregation's financial state on a regular basis. Rita and I have always believed in transparency in this area. Our former pastors were great role models in this regard.

Give, knowing that it will reproduce. I'm almost hesitant to include this because there is the potential for misunderstanding what I'm saying, misuse of what I mean, and the need for maturity to use it properly. However, it would be a bit of an injustice to shy away from the reality of the spiritual side of giving. There is a powerful aspect of the spiritual realm, whereby expectation plays a role. What you expect to get or not get can often determine the result. At the same time, it takes some spiritual maturity to understand that you are not giving precisely so you can receive. It is just the natural and expected by-product.

Case Study: Rowena

She passed away more than ten years ago, but Rowena was the poster child for what is described as "giving out of your lack." She was an original member of the congregation that Rita and I joined and later became our secretary when we became the pastors. We knew her, her children, and her grandchildren and miss her still.

Coming up, she made a bunch of bad choices with men, giving birth to four children by three different guys, none of whom turned out to be decent fathers or husbands. She ended up on public assistance in public housing as her mother had also done. Then Rowena got saved. Somehow the message of giving grabbed her heart, and she flung herself headlong into it. At first, it was a matter of making small sacrifices. She told the congregation the story of how she initially cut out buying potato chips and sodas and took a couple of dollars and put into the offering basket instead. After a few months, she was able to land a part-time job. She started to tithe even though it still meant giving up a few more things to make ends meet. A few months later, the job went full-time, and she was off food stamps. She kept giving, though, adding offerings to her tithe. Eight months or so later, she got a call from the federal government that they had an opening for her as a GS-5 (essentially entry level on the federal employment scale), with a salary equivalent of about $40,000 today. Rowena and the kids were now off both public housing and public assistance. She kept giving. Two years later, she was a GS-7 (a minor miracle, by the way, based on what she lacked in credentials), making the equivalent of $52,000. Rowena now became a homeowner. In roughly three and a half years, she went from being unemployed, hopeless, and dependent on having a stable career and being self-supporting. Rowena eventually retired as a GS-13, earning the equivalent today of about $95,000. Her story was that "I gave myself right out of poverty." She continued to give not just financially but became a deacon in the congregation and later took on the role of church secretary as a part-time job just to stay busy. Oh, and she made sure that all her kids, and even grandkids, made it to college or vocational school. She went on to be with the Lord way too soon, but she created a future for her grandchildren, who are her living legacy.

I've already addressed the tithing issue, so please don't accuse me of using this example to make a case for why you should be a tither. The point is just about giving and the reality of how it can change a person's circumstance. Let me say something, though, that you probably won't hear elsewhere. The Lord did not "bless" Rowena because she gave her money to the congregation. As a saved person, you will be blessed whether you give or not. I know that for some of you reading this, it sounds like heresy to say that, but it's true. Otherwise, your actions end up determining whether God will bless you even after accepting Jesus's sacrifice. The activation of spiritual principles produces the results of that principle. These principles are neutral and work both ways for anyone who uses them. I just thought it was important to make sure that you didn't get the wrong impression about giving. There are way too many preachers doing that already.

Have a Savings Plan

After you've taken care of giving, make sure you are able to begin a conscientious plan for saving. In some cases, your financial situation may suggest that saving might need to precede consistent giving. If this is a matter of what's required to take care of your family, then don't let anyone put you into bondage or guilt about it. Working toward consistent giving is what counts. Listening to the Holy Spirit on these matters is vital, just as Rowena's story shows.

There are various types of basic savings categories you will want to think about:

1. *Operating cushion:* setting aside three months of bills as a cushion for any fluctuations in your income or job situation.
2. *Repair/replacement fund:* Having an amount to cover the normal wear and tear of major appliances, furniture, fixtures, equipment, automobiles, clothes, etc.
3. *Stuff you want / stuff you want to do:* Saving incrementally rather than throwing down a chunk of change at one time. This calls for planning and avoiding impulsivity. (Easy for me to say, right?). Great vacations, a new car—all examples of what could be included here.

And then there are much-longer-term savings strategies for things like retirements, children's schooling, second careers, and investing. One of the biggest mistakes I think I made was not taking advantage of things like IRAs (individual retirement accounts). An IRA is a savings vehicle that gives you tax breaks for investing money for retirement. It is still an effective way to put money away for the long run. The key benefit of an IRA is that money you put in is tax-deductible up to certain levels. Not only can this help lower your taxes, but the investments in the IRA grow tax-deferred. You pay no taxes on the increase while your money stays in the account. There are different types of IRAs with slightly different features for when you can remove the money and what the tax effect will be. The overall idea is that you will be in a lower tax bracket at that point anyway. There's a lot we could get into here. Just know that it's not as complex and overwhelming as it may seem.

Protect Your Assets

To be candid, I don't like talking about insurance. There's a part of me that incorrectly feels like I am abandoning faith in seeking after protection from things that I am hoping won't happen. But we all know that things that we are expecting not to happen do.

Hearing from the Holy Spirit should supersede any analysis you hear from me or anyone else.

Insurance is also a tough business. You'd be totally shocked at a lot of the tricks and cons that can legitimately be pulled off. I say this not to denigrate insurance people. I held an insurance license for a short period of time. I say it to encourage you to do some reading and some research so that you are equipped to avoid being duped by the few less ethical people you may encounter. Regardless of the potential treachery, you need to be insured. Things like the automobile, homeowner's, renter's, and medical insurance are no-brainers. Again, this is a huge field of endeavor. Every year new insurance products are created to address all kinds of needs. I'll just cover the basics that you may choose to consider further.

Life insurance. Its main purpose is to protect your income and earning power. You need more of it in your twenties and thirties and much less in your fifties and sixties. And if you are single or don't have children, your needs are minimal as well. Don't let someone convince you to keep adding to it unless you have an objective other than income protection in mind. "Term" insurance is generally a much better deal than "whole life" insurance. Again, you'll want to do some objective research on this. Other insurances to be knowledgeable about would include the following:

Umbrella liability insurance. An umbrella policy is an extra coverage over and above what you have on your house, car, or other assets. It protects you if there is a risk of being sued for damages to someone else's property or injuries caused to someone else due to an accident. Usually, it only makes sense to have it if you have assets that you need to protect. The flip side is that coverage is relatively inexpensive. You could generally pay less than $300 a year for a million dollars of coverage.

Long-term care. Long-term care insurance is used for medical care. People benefit from it when they end up requiring home care, assisted living, adult daycare, or hospice/respite care or need to redesign their living space to accommodate their health situation. The problem is that you must purchase it when you clearly don't need it, so it's pure contingency insurance, even more so than life insurance. The experts say that the best time to go for it is in your mid-fifties. You can get very favorable rates and, most of the time, add to your coverage down the road.

Disability. This form of insurance is different from long-term care. Disability insurance replaces a portion of your income if an accident or illness, let's say, makes it impossible for you to work and earn a living. There are products that address short-term versus long-term disability and features that affect when the insurance kicks in and how long it can be received.

Whew! So I'm glad that's over. While I'll never be a fan, fortunately, I have come to that place of understanding where there is no conflict between trusting God and applying wisdom. I would also say that if there were ever situations where the value of having the Holy Spirit to consult and provide clear direction proves itself, these are those situations!

Have an Investment Plan

The pain of talking about insurance is offset by the excitement of talking about investing. We'll briefly address two areas: investing your money and investing in yourself.

Study Challenge.

Read about the "parable of the talents" in Matthew 25:14–30. It provides an insight into the concept of investing in the general sense.

There are way too many ways to invest your money than we have time and space for—the stock market, bond market, real estate, foreign currency, baseball cards, coins, stamps, cryptocurrency, precious metals, and on and on. Each will require some degree of training and education, depending on your background. It is well worth the effort to come up to speed in the areas that appeal to you. Here's the issue you will face. Do you want to learn enough about it to do it on your own, or does it make sense to have someone do it for you? Personally, I have found the answer to be both. For example, for Rita and me, it's the stock market, foreign exchange, and real estate. We spent time and money learning the mechanics and logistics. Having a background in this is what led us in this direction, of course. When it comes to real estate, we've purchased properties using our own research. When it comes to the stock market, we manage our own account with a certain sum of money at stake. At the same time, we use a professional to manage our "retirement" fund. (I have to put it in quotes because neither of us has a concept of retirement as I alluded to earlier.) Regardless of which direction you'll go, however, I'd recommend that you learn the same stuff. Being knowledgeable when it comes to your investments will make it harder for you to be scammed or to pay more than you should for advice.

You might also want to consider investing in yourself. This can range from staying up-to-date on whatever professional development is connected to your vocation, all the way to going into business for yourself. (I am totally biased in favor of being self-employed!) In between is developing and maintaining a mentality of lifelong learning, just as I suggested for your children. If you are a believer, "standing still" can be outright dangerous to your mental health. Let me take a moment and close this loop.

Study Challenge:

Read Mark 16:25–27. Think about "saving" your life in terms of not living it to the fullest.

I used to grow a lot of houseplants. I had read that they add oxygen to your living space. Back in the day, the front section of my apartment was a veritable jungle of succulents, jades, spider plants, wandering jews—you name it. I enjoyed buying small potted plants or getting a cutting from someone and then replanting them as they grew. You must pay close attention to a potted plant because although it looks pretty much the same day after day, the root system grows rapidly, looking for more nutrients. Overnight the plant will wilt nearly to the point of not being able to be revived.

Believers are in a constant state of spiritual and mental transformation, whether they choose to acknowledge it or not. In Romans 12:2, Paul equates grasping the deeper aspects of the Lord's will for our lives by recognizing that we are in a constant state of transformation. The Holy Spirit is constantly leading us into a fuller and deeper version of ourselves. I'm not talking about your external reality as much as your internal one. Staying in the same house or keeping the same job is not the issue. It's "where your head is at" as they say. It's when you stop challenging your mind and heart to grow. When you become sedentary in your personal growth and development, you will unconsciously try to hold on to that stable, consistent mental norm. The more you hold on, the more you risk becoming unhappy and not knowing why. You run the risk of waking up one day and feeling that life has passed you by. As a believer, be careful not to let the place where your mind and heart is planted become too small for the roots of your faith.

Epilogue

So there you have it. My prayer is that I have been able not only to provide you with a clear presentation of the gospel but also to accelerate your understanding of how being saved works itself out in every area of your life. I want you to know that I do try to take my own advice. I hope that as time passes, my understanding of the work of my own salvation will have grown so much, I'll have to write another book! Being saved is a journey, a daily adventure, a lifelong seat at the feet of the teacher, the Holy Spirit, a joyous thrill ride that never ends.

Shalom aleichem. May the wholeness that only comes from knowing Jesus feed you each day just like it were bread.

About the Author

LeRoy is the Senior Pastor of Global Truth Ministries in Springfield, Virginia. He is a gifted Bible teacher with a passion for revealing the truth of the innocence that Jesus provided to us by his death, burial, and resurrection. He and his wife Rita have served as missionaries in Kenya, Uganda, Mexico, and Haiti.

He has a heart for outreach and taking the message of the gospel outside the church walls. This has led to him performing jail and prison ministry, coaching collegiate sports, serving as a Fairfax County Virginia Community Chaplain, and teaching parenting and fatherhood classes. He is a certified Master Trainer for the National Partnership for Community Leadership's "Fatherhood Development Curriculum." LeRoy also conducts the Fairfax County Public Schools Family And School Partnership's "Dads Matter Class" and is a parenting program instructor for the County's Department of Family Services. He is certified in Critical Incidence Stress Management and Pastoral Counseling Intervention.

As a bi-vocational pastor, he has also operated an independent management consulting practice in corporate strategy and organizational development. His list of clients includes BMW, Citigroup, Marriott, Lockheed Martin, NASA; the U.S. Departments of Defense, Health And Human Services, Education, American Bankers Association, the Brookings Institution, Boys And Girls Clubs, United Way Of America, Energy, Treasury, State and local government agencies in California, Florida, Michigan, Mississippi, Pennsylvania, Virginia. He comments that "my consulting practice has been a huge asset to my role as a pastor. For one, I approach them both as ministry. Two, it gives me profound insight and empathy for the struggles that people face in navigating life's issue."

LeRoy is a much sought-after national and international conference speaker, award-winning author, radio, and television personality. He and Rita host the popular "Going Deep" radio program which is broadcast in more than 25 countries. His book, *Mastering the Challenges of Change*, published by the American Management Association received a Newberry Book Award and *Messages From The Mercy Seat* was published in 2012 by Joshua Tree Publishing.

LeRoy was educated at Harvard University where he received a Bachelor's degree in English and American Literature and Language, and a Master's degree in Finance and International Business from Columbia University Graduate School of Business. LeRoy received his Doctor of Divinity from Master's International School of Divinity and his PhD in Biblical Studies from Trinity Theological Seminary. He has done Talmudic studies at Yeshivat Har Etzion (Israel).

www.ingramcontent.com/pod-product-compliance
Lightning Source LLC
Chambersburg PA
CBHW022011120526
44592CB00034B/787